Peel Three

by Fred Palmer

Shore Road, Peel I.O.M.

The Leece Museum would like to thank the
Manx Heritage Foundation for their generous
assistance in publishing Peel Three.

ISBN No. 978-0-9562601-0-9

Published by The Leece Museum

Printed by The Copy Shop
Douglas

Foreword

By
Mrs Emilie Pugh (nee Palmer)

My brother Fred Palmer spent a great deal of time delving into the history of Peel. He loved Peel and if you have read any of his three previous books, Peel One, Peel Two and Glimpses of Old Peel, you will have gathered this.

The Leece Museum has decided to publish a second section of a book he never published, which I hope you will enjoy.

Many thanks to the Leece Museum and Roy Baker for doing this.

Emilie Pugh

Contents

Chapter One

The Market Place

The focal point of any community is the centre of the town, and the old centre of Peel was the Market Place, which was known as "The Crosh", and it means crossroads. Part of the area along the edge of the churchyard was called the Big Garden.

The main purpose of the market place is for the holding of markets, and so it was in Peel as it was the garrison town as well as being listed as one of the four market towns in the Island. A market was held each week, and these were supplemented by a number of fairs, the most important being the "St. Patrick's Fair", which was held on old St. Patrick's Day and its main purpose was for the hiring of female labour and also the sale of livestock, and Peel was a busy place for this fair which was the last one to be held regularly.

Regulations For Markets and Fairs

Officials appointed by the Lord of Man rigidly controlled markets and fairs, and in the case of Peel the person in charge was the Constable of Peel who was generally the officer of the garrison. Following the Revestment Act of 1765 when the English Government took over the Island, this duty was transferred to a civil administrator who was known as the Captain of Peel, he being the High Bailiff.

There are a number of regulations shown in the records governing markets, and the following are a couple of examples:-

In December, 1651, Colonel Duckenfield issued the following orders:- "Forasmuch as by an order made by the officers of this Island it is declared that the farmers and other inhabitants of the Isle furnish the markets with corn and other victuals weekly for a supply of the garrisons... I do therefore hereby require the Controller and Clerk of the Rolls to send our precept to the several parishes of the Island. The rate of corn not to be above 16/= a bowl for wheat and malt".

Then there is a later instruction just after the Revestment Act, which was, dated 1766 and read:- "The Captains of the towns among their other duties had to see that the markets were kept, the bell rung, and the market jury empanelled, that this jury presented "All forestallers, regrators, or other offenders against the laws, orders, rules and regulations, relative to markets" to "take care that in time of scarcity... no corn, provisions, or other victuals be exported... until the same be exposed to sale in the open market... at a fair price, and to ascertain that the Weights and Measures "be according to the standard."

Prices

One thing that intrigues people most, when they look at old documents, is the price of goods in comparison to the price of similar goods to-day. The following are some examples of prices during the 17th century:- In 1644 "latts" (laths, a narrow thin strip of wood used as backing for plaster or to make latticework) were sold for 1/ (5p) per 100, and ash poles for 2/6d (12 $^1/_2$ p) each. Coals were 9/3d per ton, and shot 3d. per 1lb.

Wine must have been extraordinarily cheap, for James, 7th Earl of Derby, spent one shilling on wine to give "to my Lord Nidesdaile."

The Earl of Niddessale was one of the cavalier lords who had taken refuge on the Isle of Man.

Then in 1645, barley was 9/= a bowl, and wheat 10/=. While in 1650, the price of beer and ale was 2d. per quart, and shortly after it became three pints for 2d.

Moving to December 1651, the price of wheat and malt was fixed at 16/= a bowl. The following year corn was cheaper and 15 ozs. of white bread and 21 ozs. of brown bread were ordered to be sold at 1d.

Land was cheap in 1655 as "half a quarter and 2 intackes" were sold for £6 and 7 lbs of wool. One boll (boll, a measure of 6 bushels, or 24 kishens of barley and oats, 4 bushels or 16 kishens of wheat, rye, pease, beans, and potatoes) of barley cost 63/= (£3.15p).

The value of a cow was 33/6d (£1.67p) in 1660, and at this time beef sold for 6/= a quarter, a side of mutton was 1/2d, geese 4d each, hens 2d each, eggs 1d. per dozen, butter 1/2d a 1lb and wheat at 5/= a bowl.

In 1669, £2/10/0 was paid for 18 sheep and half a cow.

A fishing boat was valued at 40/= in 1677, and another at 30/=, a horse 18/=, and a mare at 16/=.

The following prices were fixed in 1696:- wheat 14/= per bowl and the same for barley, and 9/= for oats and rye

Prices fixed in 1699, were:- barley and wheat 16/= per bowl and oats and rye 10/=.

Moving to 1721, a cow, heifer and calf sold for 30/=; horses for 12/6 each; sheep 1/= each. Five sheep and one lamb sold for 10/=; hens sold for 1/= each and a "turf spade, and English spade, and a Manks one" sold at 1/6 for the lot.

Then in 1723, a quarter of mutton cost 9½d., and a quarter of lamb 6d.; a ton of coal 14½d.; a quart of brandy 10½d.; a quart of claret 10d.; a kishen of lime cost 1d.; a web (probably 40 yards) of cloth 3½.; the same quantity of fine muslin cost 6/-; and a cotton handkerchief ¼.

A couple of years later in 1725, soap and candles cost 4½d per lb, flannel 8d per yard, course flannel 4d per yard, calamanco 13lb per yard; wine ¼d a bottle; tobacco 7d per lb; camlet 13d per yard; gloves 4d per pair; playing cards 1d per pack; cinnamon 7d per lb; saltpetre 8d per lb; pearl barley 3d per lb; silk 2/6d per yard; muslin handkerchiefs 9d each; spruce beer 2/- per gallon.

In 1738 brandy was only 1/9d a gallon; Bohea tea 4/= per lb; and green tea 3/8d. Cost of lodgings varied from 1/6d to 3/= per week; and washing linen for one-person 28/- per year.

Moving on to 1760 a barrel of lime cost 2/9d; "Fir Balk 1/6d per foot; a spade 1/9d; glue 10d a 1d; linen cloth 2/3d per yard; "frize cloth" to cover a communion table 6/- per yard; In 1798 potatoes were 8d a kishen (Kishen or Kishan - A measure containing 8 quarts equal to one peck. This was commonly used in the sale of corn, potatoes, coals, etc. In point of weight the contents of a kishan of potatoes was estimated at 21 lbs. A kishan of coals, it is said, ought to weigh 21¼lbs.) due to crop failure

Place of Punishment

The market place was not only used for markets but also for less pleasant purposes such as the carrying out of civil and ecclesiastical punishments for offences against these bodies.

The civil punishments were mainly confined to whipping, particularly in the early part of the 19th century, and an example of this is revealed in the following:- "In January, 1814, at a court of General Gaol Delivery a woman, for stealing poultry, was sentenced to be publicly whipped in Peel Market Place." This was duly carried out on February 7th. A witness who saw the event said that the man carrying out the whipping did not lay it out to heavy as he was aware of the woman's circumstances and was only stealing to feed her family as at that period of time the Island was having a difficult time and there was a lot of unemployment.

The authorities did obviously not consider the offence a serious offence either, particularly when it was compared with a youth who was charged in January, 1820, with breaking into Robert Grant's Hotel, Peel, and stealing a one pound note and a pair of shoes. For this he got transportation beyond the seas.

During the period when the ecclesiastical courts were used they appeared to be more severe with their punishments for offences against the church.

They could be classified as follows:- profaning the Sabbath, marital cases, witch-craft, slander, clerical discipline, the upkeep of church property, tithe disputes, the protection of children, the poor, the aged and insane, and all disputes regards to wills and inheritances, and it could be said it touched peoples lives from birth to grave and even beyond.

These courts treated men and women of all classes with equality. Imprisonment for any definite period of time was seldom decreed, generally the penalty was for a period of a few days to be followed by penances, and in quite a lot of cases imprisonment only came if people failed to carry out their penance.

While imprisonment "until further orders" were the fate usually of wardens who did not fulfil their obligations, or for contempt of the courts.

The ecclesiastical prison was the dungeon beneath the old St. German's Cathedral in the castle and was described by Governor Horne in 1722, to the British Government as follows;- "is a most horrid dungeon or vault under the graves in an old church in a small island in the sea".

He then went on to describe the fate of Long Jury men when three of their members failed to agree with the rest and as a result they were confined there until they reached a unanimous decision, stating:- "...Which disagreement of the said three occasioned such trouble and hazard of life to the petitioners (writing out of Peele) being several days kept in close prison without even meat, drink, firing, or candlelight, ready to perish, their feet, hands, and bodies, of times being swollen with cold, and all unable to suffer the present affliction..."

The penances varied according to the nature of offences. In most cases, the offender had to stand outside the church door for a period of time, bare armed, bare legged and footed, and without a shirt, and covered in linen all over, with a little white wand in his hand. In most cases, what he or she committed was written across the front of them.

The time chosen for this to be carried out was when the people were coming to and from church. When they had to stand on the market place as well, it was at the busiest time of a market day generally dinner time.

If the offender had been found guilty of slander, a bridle was fitted in their mouths. A Manx bridle consisted of a leather noose which was not so bad as the ones used in England. When the bridle was fitted they had to stand like the other with a notice on their chest, generally at the church and the market place.

More Pleasant Purposes

The Market Place was used for more pleasant purposes for instance it was used for public announcements, and when there was one to be made a bell ringer would go round informing the townsfolk when it was to be made and the inhabitants would assemble there to hear it. Proclamations relating to royal events were announced and assembly was at the square for special events such as celebrations for coronations etc. It was also used for open-air public meetings particularly political ones when the speakers would obtain the services of a flat cart and use it as a platform.

It was also a place where children played, and one game in particular "Smuggle Ahern". This was a kind of hide-and-seek, played in the streets at night when it was dark. The hares started off from the chosen spot and when about a hundred yards away, one of them shouted "Ahernt" and when this was heard the hounds immediately gave chase. The hares hid in doorways, dark alleys, and a favourite spot was behind the headstones in the churchyard. When a hound caught a hare he immediately shouted "AHERNT" YOU'RE CAUGHT" and all returned, and the other team went out as hares and so on.

Another favourite game was Cammag, which has similarities to hockey, with the exception that there was no limit to the players. The stick was called a cammag and it was generally gorse born, with a suitable curve in it. The ball was a crick and often a piece of cork was used as a substitute. Several choices of pitch were available from the market place, as some used from the square down Market Street, while others chose Douglas Street then there was Patrick Street and Castle Street. In these games it was generally those with plenty of beef that won as no quarter was asked or given as they lashed out at the crick.

The Market Place also had the odd occasion of excitement, one such being as follows:- "On March 9th 1887, Dr. Cole and his coachman were driving at a good pace across the Market Place, the axle of the trap suddenly snapped, causing Dr. Cole and his man, to be thrown into the street. The doctor, who was driving, did not lose possession of the reins, and the horse immediately stopped. Both escaped unhurt beyond slight shaking.

A forest of masts

Chapter Two

St Peter's Church

Overlooking the Market Place are the ruins of St. Peter's Church, a building that served Peel for almost 400 years, and was the parish church of German for about 200 years and was also the parish church of Patrick for a period. During that period the building had many facelifts, which changed its appearance inside and out.

The exact date of when the church was built seems to be unknown, but it is thought to be 1480, and the original building was probably of much simpler design, however, since it was first built it has been altered and refurbished many times.

The history of the church appears to have been lost in antiquity, but legend has it that it was built as a result of an unusual incident. One day a visitor to Peel was standing on the jetty at the entrance of the harbour watching the turbulence of the sea as it broke over the rocks of St. Patrick's Isle. As he stood there watching, a funeral party arrived on the quay and proceeded onto a ferry, which started its journey across the harbour, when halfway across, a huge wave struck the small craft and overturned it. Everybody in the boat was thrown into the sea and they all managed to scramble ashore, but the coffin was swept out to sea, and it was never seen again. Seeing this unpleasant scene, the gentleman decided that it would be much better if there was a church and churchyard in the town so he gave the money for this, and thus saved any similar accidents occurring

The earliest dated memorial stone in the churchyard was 1595, while the first entry was 1667. It must have been about this time that this church was made parish church for Patrick and German, as the cathedral on St. Patrick's Isle was only partially roofed, and generally in a poor state of repair. This is confirmed by the fact that in 1665, the wardens of St. Germans Cathedral were kept in the crypt beneath it, because they failed to obtain a price for the repair to the roof of the tower and chancel. After remaining in the crypt for a week, they appealed to the Deemster against the punishment, as they felt it was too harsh. Eventually they were released on condition that they obtained the cost of the work required to be done.

Extensive repairs were carried out in 1710 when one of the ancient low arches was removed and a deep gallery over the west wing erected with outside steps. The church was 27 yards long, the cross 19 yard 2 feet, and it had two galleries for public scholars. There was also a small ancient font.

An act of Tynwald of 1710, which was promulgated the following year, relieved the parish of Patrick of all the responsibility of upkeep of St. Peter's Church.

In the 1730's more renovations were carried out which included new pews in the south of the church and a new bell erected.

There were two inscriptions in the chancel;-
1. To captain Sylvester Radcliffe, of Knockaloe, buried December 1731, aged 78 years.

2. To Elisabeth Parr, alias Qualtrough, wife of Captain Caesar Parr, buried February 20th 1766, aged 29 years.
   There was one inscription in the church to - "John Leece, of Ballaleece, died at Knockaloe, in Kirk Patrick, July 5th. 1784, aged 27 years.

Prior to 1766 services in English were performed only once a month and all other services were in Manx. After that date services were held in Manx and English on alternative Sundays.

During 1816 extensive repairs were carried out to the church to make it more presentable to new inhabitants. At this time Peel was growing fairly rapidly.

It is also interesting to read what some people thought of the services and it also helps in making comparisons with them even if we do not necessarily agree with them. The following are two references from a diary of a newcomer to Peel in 1837:- September 3rd 1837 - The congregation was not large but attentive. The Rev. Mr. Windsor read the prayers and preached; the Vicar (Mr. Gelling) read the communion service. The singing was most horrible. The sermon, I understand was personal.

The communion silver at that time consisted of six handsome pieces; -

1. A flagon, with St. Peter's handsomely engraved thereon.

2. A very large chalice, plated, given by Lady Moore.

3. A tall chalice, inscribed, "Ecclesise Cathedralis St. German, Henricus Bridgeman, 1670." N.B. This belonged to the Cathedral.

4. A silver cup, inscribed, "The gift of John Crane, renewed by Captain Philip Cowell."

5. Another cup, silver (from the cathedral).

6. A paten, inscribed "Ex dono Henrici Bridgeman, Episc. Monensis Eccles, St. Germani," on which are the bishops arms. Ten balls, a lion pessant in chief (cathedral silver).
    Between 1860 and 1883 new communion silver was donated by Florence Gelling, of Kennaa, and comprised of:- Two patens dated 1860. A beaker dated 1863 and a chalice dated 1883.

During a visit to Peel in 1870, Mr J. K. Ward of Montreal, offered to donate a clock to the town if it was erected on the church.

This offer was duly accepted and money was raised by public subscription to build a tower to house the clock. In 1871 the old belfry was removed, and the tower erected, and the clock was duly installed in 1872.

At the same time as this work was being carried out repairs were also carried out to the church, and stained glass windows placed at the same time at the east end of the church, the gift of Misses Crellin, of Ramsey, at a total cost of £700.

Following the opening of the new church in 1884, attendances at St. Peter's Church started to decline, although it still remained the Parish Church of German until 1893. However, in the latter part of the 1890's it was decided to close the church.

In 1901 a scheme was approved by the Church Council to make the church into a non-denominational meeting room and the alterations were to be carried out within a year. This was however, not carried out and the building was still used for church purposes.

Following the great storm of 1903, it reverted back to the regular church while the new church was being repaired following the severe damage it received and this took a year. St. Peter's Church was then used as a Sunday school, and later used by the Boy's Bible Class. It was also used for lantern lectures and special services, which included those in Manx language.

However, during and after the second world war, the premises were hardly used at all, and soon the building deteriorated, and in 1958 it was decided to remove the roof and the lower walls and to make the building safe and presentable.

Chapter Three

The Peel Castle Hotel

The most prominent building on the Market Place is the Peel Castle Hotel, although the present building is only about 160 years old, there has been a public house on the site for a much longer period.

Very little is known about its early history, although on the first part of the 19th century it was advertised as an old established hotel which had a high reputation for its catering and it was also residential. The name it went under at that time was the "Peel Castle Inn."

Today it is no longer a hotel but an apartment block, refurbished by Street Heritage, a company owned by Jonathan Irving.

The building at that time was much smaller than it is today, as it only occupied half the present area and there was a private residence on the lower part of the site. In the 1830's the landlady was a widow, Mrs Thomas, she married a Mr. Edward Frissel, a lawyer, in the early 1840's, and just prior to the property being demolished they took over the old Marine Hotel in Crown Street about 1847.

When the new building was completed they moved back to the Peel Castle and continued to run it until the mid 1850's. While he was in the hotel he ran a stagecoach the "Fenella" twice a week between Peel and Douglas, and once a week to Ramsey. The stables belonging to the hotel were large ones and were on the site of the present public conveniences and shelter.

During this era, which coincided with the development of the visiting industry throughout the Island, the hotel proved to be a very popular place and was very successful. It was also used by residents in many ways, for things like banquets, social evenings and balls, as the facilities were very good as well as the catering. An example of this is revealed in the following report published on January 2nd 1886:-

Grand Fancy Dress Ball

In order to relieve the tedium and cheerlessness of our proverbial dull winter, a few local gentlemen conceived the happy idea of getting up a fancy dress subscription ball, which was accordingly held in the Peel Castle Hotel on Wednesday evening.

It was attended by the elite of the Island, and proved such a great success that it far exceeded the expectations of the most sanguine.

The ballroom was tastefully decorated for the occasion with Chinese lanterns, flags, etc., and presented such a pretty picture that it was the general theme of comment.

Some of the fancy dresses were exceedingly picturesque and tasteful and the scene in the ballroom as the dancers "tripped the light fantastic toe" to the lively strains of Mr. McNeil's string band, was brilliant in extreme. Conspicuous amongst the gay throng were three bridesmaids in wedding costumes, and who thus represented at night the character they sustained in the morning when they officiated in that capacity at the wedding of Miss Laughton, who married on the anniversary of her father's wedding day.

The ball was a most enjoyable one, and the dancing was kept up with great spirit until 4 o'clock on the following morning. During the evening, supper was provided by the urbane hostesses, Mrs. Kelly, whose catering gave universal satisfaction. The following is a list of those present, and the characters they represented:--

Anderson, Miss	Day
Anderson, Mr. J. A	Knave oof Hearts
Christian, Mrs E. H	Rouge at Noir
Corrin, Miss	Puritan Maid
Corrin, Miss A	Grecian Maid
Corrin, Mr John	Cossack Officer
Corrin, Mr T	Mexican Planter
Crellin, Miss	Chrysanthemum
Crellin, Mr	My Grandfather
Dearden, Dr	Paddy of Cork
Edwards, Miss	Eileen Aroon
Goldie, Miss	Pourdie Costume
Graves, Miss	French Lady
Graves, Mr H	Gentleman of the last century
Grave, Mr. T. J	Sir Walter Raleigh
Hill, Mr. Marcus	Magpie } Mirth
Hill, Sir Henry	Magpie } Mirth
Hodgson, Mr	Fisherman
Holt, Mrs	Watteau Costume
Holt, Mr	Coxswain of the Lifeboat
Jeffcott, Miss	Ivy leaf
La Mothe, Miss	Flower girl
La Mothe, Mr A. E	Naval Reserve Officer
Moore, Captain	Yeomanry uniform
Moore, Mrs George	Lady of the last century
Newington, Captain	Unattached uniform
Sherlock, Mr T. E	Artillery Officer
Tayleur, Mr	Wm. Shakespeare
Tayleur, Mrs	Duchess of Northumberland
Williams, Mrs	Sorrento Girl
Wilson, Mr S. H	Gentleman (year 1800)
Windus, Mrs	A Street Musician
Windus, Mr	Masher
Wood, Mrs	Catherine Di Medici
Roxborough, Dr	Chef

Besides the above there were also present the following ladies and gentlemen in evening dress, and a few names and costumes we were unable to obtain, Mrs. Dearden, Mrs Friends, Miss Fell, Miss Gell, Miss Laughton, Miss M. Laughton, Mr E. H.. Christian, Mr. Banks, Mr F. La Mothe, Mr. Lumsden and Mr. G. H. Quayle.

A Visit by the "Bounder"

The hotel was renowned for its residential and catering facilities and many famous people stayed at these premises. In 1893 a well-known journalist writing under the name of "The Bounder" for the "Clarion" paid a visit to Peel to write about its qualities as a visiting resort.

As well as writing about the beauties of Peel, such as the view from Peel Hill, the castle and other antiquities, he sometimes wrote about the people he met.

In his first article he wrote "I went and dined at the Peel Castle Hotel off a real rump steak, and a respectable bottle of St. Julian; and then went a-nooning on the Castled steep, where all earthly and sordid cases vanished from my immediate purview. And as I was sensible since leaving London ten summers had been depleted from my tale of years. But yes. It was very brave."

In another article "I met a learned Manx Philologer at the Peel Castle Hotel who informed me that the "Three Legs of Man" were not derived from the ancient tri-forked giant whom St. Patrick drove into the sea, but a Sicilian family, who intermarried with the Monarchical folk of Norway. But he didn't vouchsafe to explain the raison d'etre of the three legs. When I pressed this question home, he showed me a curious optical delusion by putting sixpence in a basin, which was invisible - I mean the sixpence. Then he poured water into the basin, until the sixpence was visible. He was no relation to the landlady, but his name was Kelly. I asked him what he meant by wasting such a lot of good water. But he stinted and said naught. The Manxmen have not a prehensile or nimble imagination - they are not swift of apprehension.

Two more parties by the name of Kelly came in, one from Ramsey and the other from Castletown. They talked of crops in English and then quarrelled in Manx. It appeared to be a language of "Q's" and "X's" and my only wonder is that their back teeth were not worn out.

I may observe, as a student of Comparative Anatomy, that as the cats have no tails, it is only fair to presume that the men have no back teeth. This is quite as reasonable and inferences as some of those, which are adduced in Tory leaders concerning the coal, strike. It is also within the bounds of fair comment.

But the Manx women - Ah!

At this juncture I found I had only 4¹/₂d. left, so I went to the Postmaster, who was also the apothecary, and wired for another hundred. Until the arrival of which I solaced myself with the guidebook. H'm! These High Church dignitaries seemed to have carried on the same old game in little Manxland as in the greater states. How is this for low?

In a panegyric of Bishop Wilson we read - Here Bishop Wilson, "Whose praise in all churches" was enthroned, April 11th 1698. But in spite of his many excellences, he was a rigorous disciplinarian, and in church matters imbued with the dominant spirit of that period.

In 1710, the Clerk of the Rolls, refusing to pay the amount claimed of him for tithes, the Bishop confined him to a dungeon and rejected the prisoner's petition to be heard in his own defence as not customary. "not customary" is delicious.

In another article the "Bounder" met a philologer and is "Witched"

"One of the most curious peculiarities of the Isle of Man is that originally all the natives were called Kelly. This cognomentary sameness resulting in any confusion, a few changed their names, but nine-tenths of the Islanders are still called Kelly, the more respectable, or higher caste being distinguished by the prefix "Hi" - "Hi-Kelly's." "Hi" being, as a learned Manx Philologer, with whom I foregathered at the Peel Castle Hotel explained, a contraction of the "High." The Hi-Kelly's of the Island are High-Kelly's and have no connection with the "Derby-Kelly's" who are purely an English branch of the family, expatriated many centuries ago.

2 Douglas Street

On the site of the Milan Veterinary Practice, 2 Douglas Street, were the Duke of Atholl's Stables and this was bought by Dumbell's Bank in 1871 when the present building was erected and it reflects what local craftsmen could do with local stone. Following the collapse of Dumbell's Bank in 1900, the premises were taken over by Parr's and they continued to use it as a bank. Later it became Westminster Bank and when Westminster merged with the National Bank it became Nat/West, these premises were sold and became the Post Office. When the Post Office moved premises in October 20th 1995 the building was later let to the Milan Veterinary Practice.

Other Buildings

The buildings in close proximity to the churchyard, all have strong associations with the Graves family. The little shop and house by the gate is where their business as merchants began. The house with the outside staircase was their family home until 1783, and later became their sail room. The house alongside was also built by them and was resided in by one of the family.

Chapter Four

The Mill Road Area

Moving from the Market Place to Station Road (which was formerly known as the "Well Brow") and originally lead from Patrick Street to the Big Well past the Garey Brown. The road was renamed by an order in 1874 signed by the High-Bailiff, Robert Moore.

PL. 61. 'Gladys'

Patrick's Well

Patrick's Well or "Chibbyr Pherick" was situated halfway down the left hand side and it was often referred to as the "Big Well" and was the one used by people living in the area of Patrick Street, Market Place, Castle Street, Church Lane, Lake Lane, etc. It was regularly used by people in this area until the 1880's, and in times of drought people went to this well as early as 4 o'clock in the morning to ensure of a days supply of water. When water was piped to the houses the well was made into a flushing tank for the sewers along the quay, and this was used regularly up to the 1960's. However, during the 1970's it was filled in, and this removed the last public well in Peel.

Lake Lane

Lake Lane is the lane leading from Market Place to Station Place, just before Station Road. Like many other streets in Peel it did not have a proper name and took it from the person living in it. It was renamed in 1874 and took its name from the lake, which was still in existence at that time on the site of the boat park. The lane originally was very narrow and only one person could pass along it at a time, particularly if they were ladies wearing old-fashioned dresses. Two of its better-known names were Tom Dawson's Lane or Nan Siddleton's Lane, both of these people ran the public house in the street during the early part of the 19th century. The building they occupied is still standing today it being a single fronted house with a large garden halfway down on the right hand side.

Peel Gasworks

At the junction of Mill Road with Station Road was the Peel Gasworks. This company was formed in 1851 and an Act of Tynwald dated 1857 governed its operations. At that time the company consisted of 300 £5 shares. It was developed successfully during the early period as at that time Peel was very prosperous through the fishing and the town was growing rapidly. In 1907 a new coal fired plant was installed, and during the 1920's an additional storage container was installed.

With the advances in electricity, the company, like others on the Island, ran into difficulties and to continue to provide the public with a service the Manx Government gave assistance and eventually in 1967 took over the operations of the company. To make the operation more viable the butane gas system was installed in 1971. Then in November 1983, the first steps back into privatisation were taken when "Calor Gas" took over.

An interesting feature of the old coal fired building is that the stone used was Peel slate with red brick. The slate is very hard, and if closely inspected, the chisel marks when the stone was being cut and dressed can still be seen.

The Graves Warehouse

Filling a large area of Station Place and occupying the area between Lake Lane and Station Road is a large warehouse which was erected by the Graves family and was used to store the ropes, sails, etc., which they had made and also the materials for making the goods.

In the early part of the 20th century the building was sold, and since then has been used for many purposes. During the early 1900's it was used as the Peel Town Commissioners Office. However, various seed merchants, the last of whom was Mr. W. Kelly, used the major portion of the building. In more recent times the building became the property of Messrs. N. R. Corlett Ltd. who used it as a warehouse for their products of concrete tiles, pipes, etc.

The building lay dormant for many years and today it has been transformed into a luxury apartment building.

The Old Smithy

The old smithy used by the Graves family business for the iron fittings for the ships they built, was part of what became the Gasworks and was in the sandstone building alongside the road. The Graves family particularly in the early part of the 19th century built a large number of clinker type boats, and for this riveting was very much part of this, hence the smithy and during the 1850's five blacksmiths were employed by them in this smithy.

When the Graves family gave up shipbuilding in 1897, the smithy was taken over by the Watterson family, who occupied these premises until the late 1920's, when they moved to the quay, and the building was taken over by the Gasworks for storage purposes.

Graves Timber Yard

The Graves family were originally merchants and when shipbuilding developed on a large scale in Peel they set up a timber yard and this was situated alongside the Gasworks in Mill Road. The family ran this for well over 80 years. The census returns for 1851 show that Henry Graves, timber merchant, employed 36 men, and the foreman at that time was his brother James Graves. The sawmill, which was part of this establishment, employed seven men.

There was also a barkhouse on the premises which was used for the darkening and preserving of fishing net, and this was the last premises in which this operation was carried out in Peel.

Behind the building and still standing, although it has not been used for over 100 years is an old chimney, unfortunately no one appears to know what it was really used for and even old records are vague. Some thought it was for some sort of factory while others thought it was to do with the early barkhouse. However, it still remains standing and will be an arguing point as long as it remains.

In 1904 the Graves family sold the yard and business, and it was purchased by W. O. Quayle who continued to run the yard successfully until the early 1950's when the building was converted into a fish-processing factory for Seabourne fish processors and were the last business to use it. The building was later sold to the Manx Government. The building was demolished in 1997.

It is an interesting note that two riverboats were built by Mr. Kermode (father of Bob and George) in this yard. These vessels were built for the British Government in 1919 for the use on the River Nile. An interesting feature was that they were built purely of Manx timber.

Salt Field

Just above the old timber yard was a field now occupied by many of the fish processors, was a field known as the "Salt Field". It got its name as this was the site of many open-air curing stations that came to Peel for the herring season. As a result of the constant use of brine in the area, even the grass wouldn't grow, hence the name.

Near the timber yard was a low building where the tar was melted for putting on the ropes and nets, a process carried out right up to the early part of the 19th century when it was made law that nets and ropes had to be barked. The nets or ropes were spread out on the field and the tar was brushed onto them. This resulted in a large amount of tar being placed on the ground, and in some areas there could be found several inches of tar.

Boat Suppers

This field was also used regularly for the carrying out of an old custom associated with crew suppers. Each year at the end of the herring-fishing season every boat held a supper for the crew. It was called the "Boat Supper" or " Shirrer Burt Beatey or Sooley." The object of the supper was for the sharing out of the final sum left after all the expenses had been cleared, and also for the hiring of crew for the next season.

The occasion was a very special one and the men generally brought along their wives and sweethearts. The meal consisted of Manx fare :- bonnags, soda cakes, potato cakes, bun loaf, apple tarts, and so on, plus the joogh (a barrel of ale and a jar of rum, which flowed like water).

These suppers were not held on any special date, and they appeared to be spread out from the end of the herring season in October to the end of January. However, one of the most popular days was St. Stephen's day. It has been known that some of these celebrations for crews have lasted as long as three days, and there are odd occasions when one of the crew has continued the celebration for seven days.

The proceeding opened with a meal, and this was followed by the share out of the remainder of the money earned during the season. The skipper handed out a shilling to his best man, naming the conditions, and the shilling was passed to the next man, and so on, until all the crew were engaged. When it reached the last man, he put the shilling into a quart measure, and then tossed it into the air, and turned the mouth under, if it came up heads it was considered lucky. The man then handed the shilling back to the skipper, and in doing so, told him that the crew expected him to conduct himself in an honest and proper manner as became a skipper, towards the owner and the crew.

A musician was then brought in, and the evening became lively with plenty of singing and dancing. Any of the crew members who could perform, did so, as did their wives, and the items were interspersed with dancing.

This went on until all the "Joogh" was gone, and then the crew performed the final act before departing for home. This consisted of a re-enactment of the letting out of the nets and then hauling them back in again. To do this the crew went into a field, and the most popular field was the "Salt Field" when they went they brought with them an oar, a barrel, and a piece of net. The skipper would place the oar in a gap in the hedge, then sit on the barrel, and mimed steering the boat. In the meantime the crew proceeded to pass the net over the hedge, where two other members of the crew ran it out, and for the hauling in the procedure was reversed.

The crew also went through the procedure of proving in between, as if they were actually at sea, even to the normal conversation they carried on during their actions. Some even took the ceremony further by having a man over board, and going through the various motions of launching a small boat, and rescuing the man.

When this was completed most of those present went home, but there were some who like to continue the celebration even for days.

This field was also used for other purposes, it has been used for several seasons as a football pitch when major repairs were being carried out on the original field.

During the 1950's the Manx Government built a number of fish processing houses with the object of moving those in the town to here, and now that has been completed. Since then there have been a number of extensions and the area has been further developed to suit modern needs.

The Brickworks

As Peel grew throughout the 19th century it was only natural that there should be a brick manufacturer in the town to replace the old and more expensive method of using stone. In 1884 it was announced that a company had been formed for this purpose and it was not long before the buildings for the manufacture of bricks were erected on a site near the railway station in Mill Road, and it was not long after that a siding directing into the yard was made so that bricks could be loaded onto goods wagons for their transportation to other parts of the Island.

The bricks were made of clay and the shale for their manufacture was obtained from a quarry a few hundred yards away at the bottom of Peel Hill. To obtain this a special bridge was built across the River Neb and flat iron rails were laid between the quarry and the works to take the clay to the works from the quarry. The trucks were drawn by horses and as the quarry got deeper and went below the level of the river, an engine and pump were installed to keep the quarry free of water and also to haul the trucks up the side to the top.

The company proved to be a success and employed large numbers of men from Peel on a regular basis. During the First World War the company expanded and went into the cheaper form of cement brick against the kiln hardened brick. However, this venture was not as successful as anticipated and did not operate for very long. In more recent times an attempt was made to re-open this plant to compete with modern brickworks, but the equipment was old and no longer efficient enough to compete against other more modern cost efficient companies.

Then in the latter part of the 1920's new kilns were erected along with a new chimney. The company was run with reasonable success and from time to time during periods of recession had to close until more bricks were required.

During the 1930's the venue of the quarry changed to a site just beyond Glenfaba Bridge and an access road to the brickworks was made from Patrick Road to allow lorries an easier access and relieve the traffic in Mill Road.

The firm managed to tick over during the Second World War, and was kept busy for the period just after when there was a lot of building going on. There was a recession in the mid 1050's and the company closed for a time, but re-opened in time for the building boom that followed.

However the Peel Brick Company started to receive very keen competition from more modern forms of building and cheaper. As the equipment was old fashioned and needed complete modernisation and as the cost of this was beyond the company, it was decided to sell the works. However, the new company got caught up in the recession in 1980, and this resulted in some of the land being sold to the Isle of Man Electricity Board who demolished the chimney. Following this the plant closed down altogether.

The Chemical field

The field beyond the "Salt Field" was known as the "Chemical Field" taking its name from the Chemical Works that occupied part of the field. Little is known of its early history but it is thought it opened in the late 1860's or early part of the 1870's to manufacture fertilizers, and sold oils for engines and machinery and nets, colza, mineral, linseed (boiled or raw), sperm, oliver and lard; grease-cart, strap, water wheel, cog wheel, and mill; Varnishes - black ship, black for iron, red oxide, brown or green, lamp wick, cotton waste, Brunswick black, coal tar pitch, resin, petroleum oil and spirit, tallow, soft soap, burning Naphite, solvent, sulphate of ammonia and sulphate of ammonia manures, solid asphalt for barn and warehouse floors, yards, etc, the cheapest and most durable flooring that can be used, prevents damp and rodents getting through.

The business ran until the 1890's when it appeared to go out of business, and it was not very long before the building got into a ruinous state. During the years it was in operation, it seemed to trade under three different names - "Mona Chemical Works", " Isle of Man Chemical Works" and the "Isle of Man Chemical and Gas Products Company, Limited".

The latter name was brought about through a prospectus on October 4th, 1884, and consisted of £18,000 in 6,000 shares of £3 each. The company had been formed for the purpose of purchasing the "Isle of Man Chemical Works Company, Limited," and for the completion and further extension of the works, and for the developing of the business on a much larger scale.

The business then conducted, consisted of distillation of gas tar and Ammoniacal Liquor, and the manufacture for Salts of Ammonia, Pitch, Naptha, Benzole, Anthracine, Creosote, Oils, Greases, Varnishes and other Gas Residuals, and for which there is a great demand and ready market.

At that time the works, plant and machinery were valued at the sum of £7,710, and was intended to make the transfer of all this on the 1st day of November of the year.

It also stated that the company had entered into several large and important contracts for the purchase of raw materials and the sale of manufactured products, all of which would be handed over to the new company. The engineer and chemist was Mr. Thomas Henry Davis, a Fellow of the Institute of Chemistry, London.

The company appeared to be doing very well that year and the following is an example of some of the goods that were exported from the Works and was published on October 25th 1884: -

"CHEMICAL COMPANY   - This company has been shipping manufactured products rather heavily this week, two schooners and their steamer having been despatched with goods for the chemical markets, the value of which we have heard pronounced was nearly £1,000."

Chapter Five

Close Chairn

The area between the harbour bridge, Glenfaba Road, and the Patrick Road is known as "Close Chairn" and in the translation of Kneen's Place Names it means "Lords Land" or Bishops Land. It is difficult to ascertain whether the land belonged to the Bishop or Church, but there is definite evidence that it did belong to the Lord of Man at that time of the Revestment Act and later as it is shown on Corris's Map of 1784 as Duke of Atholl's land.

For a very long period most of the area was used as farmland and the most recent house belonging to the farm is still standing with the water tower alongside it, and it went under the name of "Close Chairn". Just below the Glenfaba Bridge the River Neb divided into two and a small river or stream ran on the other side of the old railway line and joined the main river again just above the harbour bridge, and in places the old course is still visible. This tributary was cut off when the railway was built.

There are many stories associated with the farmer who lived there during the middle of the 19th century and the following are a few examples:- "Juan Yower worked on "Close Chairn" for the late Mr. Carran. One dark winter's morning Juan turned into work rather late, and was brought to task by his master, who said the days are very short now," "Well" said Juan, "If they are short, they are as thick as ever they'll be." Mr Carran retorted, "If you will give me any more of thy impudence, thou will get a change of porridge." "Thank God for that," said Juan "It was middlin thin yesterday."

"Sid Philip, one of the worthies living in Peel many years ago, was engaged in setting potatoes in a field adjoining the highroad. This was in the days when it was in the fashion to change the kind of potatoes planted very often. "What sort of potatoes are you setting?" asked an inquisitive neighbour. "Raw ones," replied Phil."

"The Mr Carran aforementioned, bought an Irish horse, Juan Yower, as soon as he had taken charge of the animal, commenced speaking to it in Manx. Mr. Carran, said to Juan, "Speak English to the horse man - the horse doesn't understand you." " I only know two or three words of English without going to waste them on a horse." Was the quick retort from Juan.

Used for Sporting purposes

One of the uses made of this area was horse racing and the following reflects this:- There appeared in the "Manx Advertiser" of March 30th.1811, an announcement for an event Easter Monday, April 15th 1811.

Horse Races at Peel

On Easter Monday a given prize of two saddles, value five guineas, will be given for the first horse home, the best of two three-mile heats. Entrance, one shilling to the pound, for any horse that never was known to win the sum of ten pounds, catch weight.

Any gentleman who wishes to enter a horse must apply before 11 o'clock. In the afternoon, a sweep for ponies fewer than eleven hands high. Entrance, half-a-crown. The prizes, which will be lodged in the hands of two respectable gentlemen of the town, will be advertised on the post.

Excellent Sport

The press of that period said that these races "afforded most excellent sport, and attracted a greater concourse of people than there has been remembered an any occasion whatever."

The Card

In 1813, horse racing on the Island flourished more than ever. On Easter Monday, at Peel, there was a number of races ran. These per card were as follows: -

1. For horses - a saddle, value three guineas, and a bridle, value three guineas
2. For horses that never raced before - a saddle, value three guineas
3. A pony for a bridle and whip
4. A sweepstake for a beaten horse
5. A pair of breeches, raced for by men in sacks
6. Three yards of linen, run for by women
7. Six pounds of tobacco grinned for
8. A pig, run for

Great Sport

The "Isle of Man Weekly Gazette" of April 22nd that year, gave the following extra-ordinary account of these sports: -

"In the second heat for the Maiden Plate, the horses had not run half a mile before one of the jockeys (Paddy), who rode Lord Doelittle's horse, was thrown into a dangerous position by the saddle slipping. His feet having quitted the stirrups, he actually held the saddle with one hand.

He lost that heat; to console him a subscription purse hit was handed to him containing three and sixpence.

The sweep was run for (course, one mile, horses rode by gentlemen) by the following thoroughbred mares: - Mr. C . . . tt's "Long Back," Mr. H . . . d's "Physic," Rev. Mr. M . . . d's "Mountaineers."

They went off at score, and continued neck and neck for the chief part of the heat, when Mountaineer won by a length and a half. Many hundreds were depending on this race, though the mares were all "broken winded."

Most of the nobility and fashionable of the Island attended the course, and the banks of each side of the course were filled with beauty and elegance

The ordinary at Grants Liverpool Coffee House was sumptuous, and conviviality was the order of the day.

At the beginning of the 20th century, it appears that horse racing was back in popularity again as revealed in the following article published on July 11th 1903: -

Horse Races at Peel

On Monday there was held at Peel for the first occasion the Manx Hunt Club races. The course was laid out on several fields on Close Chairn, through the ruined chemical works, which were a serious obstruction, but an adequate way had been levelled through, making, generally speaking, a fair run of about half a mile. Lying in a hollow, the ground was easily overlooked from Peel Hill and Patrick Street, and hundreds of spectators viewed the races from these vantage points instead of paying for entrance to the course. Still, a large crowd passed the gates, and the club is said to be satisfied with the financial results. A start was made with the races at three o'clock, when the following events were run:-

HACK RACE, Flat, for horses and ponies belonging to businessmen - twice round the course.

    1. W. Watsons "Mountain Boy";

    2. Arthur Roney's "Manx Queen";

    3. Ben Kinvig's "Annie Laurie."

TYNWALD PLATE (Flat), Open - Three times round the course.

    1. R. Gouldes's "Lucy";

    2. T. S. Atkinson's "Cherry Ripe";

    3. Dutton's "Genevieve";

    4. Matthew's "Honest John."

MEMBER'S RACE, for member's of the Hunt Club only.

    1. Mabbott;

    2. Smith;

    3. Daly

PONY RACE, for ponies 14 hands and under.

    1. R. Cain's "Nora";

    2. E. Dutton's "Sceptre."

FARMERS RACE (Flat), for Horses belonging to Farmers and Owners of not less than 50 acres, and which the Isle of Man Harrier's are allowed to hunt. - Twice round the course about one mile

    1. R. Goulde's "Lucy";

    2. H. Macbeth's "Sybil";

    3. W. Watson's "Mountain Boy."

Honest John jibbed at the start, but at last got away, Sybil leading. Sybil was jumping beautifully, and leading for about 20 yards after the first round, when, for some reason, the starter stopped the race. In the meantime Honest John had gone three-quarters round when he took a hedge instead of a hurdle, and the jockey fell on some stones. He was badly cut about the head, but after a while recovered, and was able to walk off the course. The reason why the horses had been pulled up was not very apparent, but it was very hard lines on Sybil, who had just, come out of another race. A fresh start had been made, when Lucy won by four lengths.

FARMER'S RACE (Flat), for horses not belonging to farmers of not less than fifty acres, over which the Isle of Man Harriers are allowed to hunt, (owner to ride).

1. Ben Kinvig's "Annie Laurie;
2. T. E. Jefferson's "Bobby"; W. Quayle H. K's "Betty"; F. Crowe's "Black Bess."

Annie Laurie won by two lengths. After the race Mr. Kinvig was thrown, but not seriously hurt.

STEWARD'S RACE (Flat), for Stewards that have acted the same during the races. First prize presented by the President; second, presented by the judge; third, presented by the starter. Messrs. Mabbott, Daly, Smith, Cubbon, F. Crowe and Capt. Ponsonby started. Daly and Mabbott raced neck and neck for half the distance, when the latter ran out, and Daly won, Smith being second, and Crowe third.

The following were the officials - President, J. C. Bason, C. P, Vice President, Mr H. Macbeth; committee and mounted stewards, Messrs. A. Rigby, A. R. Stacey, F. O. Mabbott, G. Elliot, J. Cubbon, Jun., J. B. Egner, W. W. Sandbrook, J. Clarke, Jun., W. J. Moore, A. Moore, W. Spittal, W. T. Smith-Piercy, J.C.Dixon, C. Teare, W. Kennaugh, R. Cain, Dr. Williams, W. Gold, W. Burrows, J. Smith, R. Gelling, W. Marsden, Capt. Ponsonby, J. J. Taggart, T. E. Jefferson, T. J. Bridson, C. Morfitt, F. Frost, Newton, Cook, J. G. Corrin, H. Quayle, E. E. Newham, G. Sayle, E. E. Christian, Sam Dale, D. Driver, J. Cowley, F. Crowe, Walker, Anderson, E. Dawson, and Heywood Daly; Judge, Councillor R. Moore, Starter, Mr. Joseph Clarke; hon. veterinary surgeon, Mr. H. Race; hon. secretary and treasurer, Mr W. J. Corkill; and assistant hon. secretary, Mr. W. Spittal.

Archery

One of the favourite pastimes of the early 19th century was archery. Peel had a very good team of archers who shot regularly against other teams from parts of the Island and one of the regular sites they used was Close Chairn.

During the latter part of the 19th century when the area was being broken up for other purposes, part of the land was used as a rugby pitch, and another area for football, and sometimes other sports.

Engineering

When the land was broken up, the farmhouse also changed its use and was used for a wide range of things. One was an engineering works and some fine things were developed here such as engines to drive steam capstans, and especially treadle net making machines.

In 1904, Mr. Philip Moore, an engineer and machinist, had his works in Close Chairn. He invented a treadle operated net making machine. During the period he was testing and improving the machine, he received orders to make mackerel nets for Mr. W. E. Teare's boats and completed the order successfully. This was followed by orders from Scotland and Ireland.

During the same period Mr. Moore built several more of these machines and operated them by a steam engine. At this time the only other net factory operating in Peel, the Gourock Ropework Company Limited, who by 1908 had transferred all their machinery and the staff to operate them to Scotland, leaving Mr. Moore as the only net maker.

The looms he made had a drum about 2 feet 6 inches in diameter with large pedals in front, and each time the pedals were pressed and a lever pulled a line of nets was made.

In 1909 Mr. Moore sold some of his machines to Mr. W. E. Teare who set up his own net making factory on the quay. Mr. J. J. Joughin also bought some of the looms and re-opened his factory in Stanley Road, which had been closed since 1904, following the death of his father.

Mr. Moore's house and grounds in more recent times was used as a holiday camp for tents and this was run successfully up to the

Second World War. In the early 1950's the land including the house was purchased for the erection of the Island Power Station, the house is still standing and is one of the houses occupied by the employees at the station.

Rope Works and Walk

During the 19th century a large portion of the Lord's Land was absorbed for commercial purposes. The industry occupying the furthest extremity of the land was the Ropeworks and Walk. It was in a building on the banks of the River Neb just past the Power Station, and the walk ran along side the millrace. Although there is very little of it left at present as in recent years the Electricity Board have been using modern equipment to keep the race clear by travelling along the walk.

This was one of the many enterprises run by the Graves family and appears to have started early in the 19th century about the same time as the great development in shipbuilding.

The building was of slate but all that remains of it is a patch of rubble. The roof was wooden, covered with felt, and the roof was destroyed by fire in the 1880's and then replaced with corrugated iron.

With the large amount of shipbuilding, which took place in Peel during the 19th century, as well as the development of the fishing it could be taken for granted that this was a success as the ropes were of good quality. In the 1850's there were twenty-three people employed here. An unusual feature of this works was the rope walk, which was 1,000 feet long and was between two walls but was without a roof. The ropes were spun by machinery, and as it was twisted the men had to back along the walk keeping it taut.

The widths of the ropes varied from one inch to six inches. The heavy ropes were used for moorings, and the thinnest for the tops and bottoms of nets and for Dandy rigging. This firm gained a diploma in the International Fisheries Exhibition in London for their thin rope.

The lengths varied from 35 fathoms for small ropes to 120 fathoms for the large ones. The bulk of the heavier ropes were exported and a large proportion of the inch ropes were used for nets in Peel. The exact date of when the rope works closed is unknown, but it is thought it is probably in the late 1890's most likely about the same time as the shipyard closed. At this time the fishing industry was well on the decline and Henry Graves health was also failing.

Cooper Mill

The building that is above what is now known as the Peel Town Commissioners yard, was once a flour mill, and was about one hundred years ago known as Cooper's Mill, taking its name from a former owner, Charles Cooper. However the mill is shown on Corris's Map of 1784, as belonging to the Duke of Atholl.

It was originally driven by a water wheel fed directly from the millrace, which ran alongside the building to the wheel, which was being driven. However, when the mill came into private ownership the building was completely rebuilt and also a dam put alongside to ensure a more constant supply of water.

Charles Cooper appeared to run the mill very successfully, and this was revealed when he died in May 1811, at the age of 68 years, he bequeathed the property at a figure above £60 per annum for the poor of Peel. Mr. Cooper's will dated 23rd November 1810, left a dwelling house in Peel (Castle Street), yards and water corn mill, of annual chief rent of £2, to be held by Philip Moore and John Gell, in trust, and to allow his wife, Ann, possession during her life, or so as she remained unmarried.

The mill was to be subjected to an annuity of £20 to the Vicar and Wardens of German for the Poor of Peel, during his wife's life or widow-hood; and upon her death to convey the house and mill to the wardens, with the condition that should the wardens neglect to keep the mill, etc., in proper repair the heir-at-law to possess himself of the property.

The mill continued to run for many years after this, and was also used for special occasions. As the majority of the fishermen were crofters, and as the fishing season did not finish until well after the harvest, women and girls, who also did the sheep shearing, did the reaping. When the harvest was completed a Mhellia was held.

In Peel some of the crofters and farmers held their celebrations in Cooper's Mill, as there were no halls in Peel at that time. Here young and old assembled for supper, plus a song and dance. One such event was held in the mill in 1837 as written by a diarist of the time. After giving a description of a Mhellia, he went on to say that when the fiddler engaged for the occasion it would be nice to have some music from the mill opposite.

At that time there was no bridge across the harbour at that point as there is today, only a ford with stepping-stones. While crossing the river on these stones, he slipped, and away went the fiddle down the stream. The diarist on seeing the commotion as he was passing by, enquired of the cause, and when told, turned to the musician saying "I pity your case, poor man." "Pho" said Charley the fiddler, "to the devil with the case, it's the fiddle I want."

Threshing at the time was done by hand, and it was the usual thing in the winter months to do the threshing by means of flails. Men, who were not occupied on the fishing during the winter months, generally did this.

In the 1840's the Glenfaba Mill was opened and as it was more easily accessible, it probably took a great deal of business from Cooper's Mill. This resulted in it eventually being closed down, and the premises were empty for a number of years before it was leased by Mr. T. Watson and converted into a sawmill.

Chapter Six

Watson's Shipyard

One of the most successful shipyards in Peel during the latter part of the 19th century was Thomas Watson's yard in Mill Road. It was situated on the site now occupied by the Peel Town Commissioners yard, which lies between Moore's fish yard and the old mill on the banks of the River Neb. He along with all the other shipbuilders in Peel, built many of the new vessels for the expanding Peel fishing fleet during the 1870's, reaching it's peak during 1878-79. At that time there was a low footbridge across the harbour just below the bridge at the top of the harbour so that when boats were launched they had to be dragged to the bridge before they went into the water. His workshop at that time was a large hut near the fish yard.

Although many fine fishing vessels were built in the yard, his real speciality was the building of real top class yachts that were greatly admired for their speed and fines lines, and throughout the years many of these were exported.

Unfortunately there is not much information available about the early part of the business, although details of the later part of the business life of the firm including its expansion are available which reflects its ups and downs.

'Manx Princess'

On May 14th. 1883, Mr. Watson launched a yacht which was christened the "Fly". It was 30 feet in length with and 8 feet beam, and was cutter rigged, and had a false keel to allow more cabin space. It was built for Mr. Ashburner, of Manchester.

Then on May 22nd. 1883, a vessel was launched for the purposes of fresh fish buying. She had a 34 feet keel.

New Workshop

Then in October, 1883, Mr. Watson, took over Cooper's Mill, which was just above his own yard, and had been unattended for a long time. The whole of the corn mill appliances were removed, and the inside fitted up as a large workshop and stores. The waterpower that had previously operated the corn mill drove the corn mill, and included in the equipment was a modern planning machine, all the alterations were carried out in eleven months, and the premises became operational in September 1884.

Work Continued Throughout Alterations

While the new workshop was being fitted out work in the shipyard continued. On February 27th 1884, two luggers were launched. One was the "Geraldine," 47 feet Keel, 15 feet beam, completed with all fittings, having oak grained cabins, commodious berths, cooking stoves, etc., and its destination was Glendower. The other lugger was the same measurements and its destination was Cape Clear.

During a fresh breeze from the south on March 13th. 1884, the new lugger "Geraldine" of Glendower, was taken out on her maiden trip, and the crew were highly pleased by the manner in which she behaved.

Then it was recorded on May 16th. 1885 - "In the yard of Mr. T. Watson, boat-builder, there may now be seen two handsome yachts which this energetic and enterprising builder has almost ready for launching. Both are beautifully modelled, and one at least is likely to give a good account of herself in any race in which she may be engaged.

The smaller of the two crafts is to be used as a pleasure boat at Port Erin, but the larger one, which is being built for Mr. Watson's sons, will continue to hail from Peel.

Then on June 12th. 1885, a splendid lugger was launched, being built for owners in the South of Ireland.

A splendid yacht was launched on June 19th 1885, which is expected will give a good account of herself at forthcoming regattas.

He Expands Across the River

Business appeared to be very brisk at this period so it was only natural to see an expansion of the business. It was recorded on May 14th 1887, that Mr. Thos. Watson, shipbuilder, had purchased from G. P. Quayle, Esq., the whole of the frontage of Peel Hill, adjoining Peel river, running from the boundary of the field lately owned by Mr. David Dodd, to a small house formerly used as an office by the Peel Slate Quarry Company. Mr. Watson excavated the plot and made it level and prepared for shipbuilding.

The following appeared on March 10th 1888. - It was reported that Messrs. T. Watson and Co.; have the contract for building of a steamer 90 feet long and above 100 feet over all. She is to be built to the order of a gentleman in Douglas for the purpose of pleasure, and the work will commence at once.

On April 26th 1888 a dougle* rapid progress is being made with the pleasure steamer now being built for Douglas. The firm appears to have plenty of work on hand.

*Dougle or Daagan. An old nickname (now obsolete) in Peel for a fishing-smack

The steamer was launched on June 26th 1888. It was the twin-screw "Mermaid," intended to run trips from Douglas to Port Soderick, the Calf and other places. She was built to the order of Messrs. Knox and Co., of Douglas. Mr. Knox performed the ceremony of naming the vessel.

In a few days the vessel will be brought to Douglas to have her engines placed in her. As the vessel glided from her fastenings, Mr. T. Quayle, who was on deck, fell against the bulwarks and received some injury. He had to be carried home, and the doctor attended to his injuries. We are pleased to learn, however, he now able to walk out again.

While all the other shipyards appeared to be having a lean time the following news item was published on April 20th 1889.

It is pleasing to note that notwithstanding the unprecedented dullness in almost every branch of the industry in town, Mr. Thomas Watson, is at present busily engaged in putting up three boats, viz, a nobby, a pleasure boat and a trawler.

It was recorded on January 11th 1890, that he had launched a fine nobby, which will take up the long-line fishing in a few days, and will join the herring fleet in the summer.

Then on January 24th 1890, Mr Watson launched a nobby for Mr. Thompson, of Girvan, who will take her to that port and fit her out for the approaching mackerel fishing.

On Tuesday 11th 1890, he launched a further nobby.

It was announced on March 22nd 1890, that Mr. Watson received an order for a new schooner to carry 150 tons, to be ready by the end of August next. Captain Charles Gill, late of the "Annie Cowley" is to take command.

A report of April 26th 1890 revealed there was in the course of construction in this yard, a steam ferryboat 60 feet long, 16 feet beam, and 7 feet deep, with a carrying capacity for 400 passengers.

This vessel was launched during the week ending June 21st 1890, and will be used for ferry traffic between Victoria and Battery Piers, and built to the order of Messrs. Knox, engineers, Douglas. She was named "Jingo" and was towed to Douglas for the engines to be fitted.

There were also problems with launchings and the occasional accident as was revealed in the following newspaper report dated January 9th 1892.

Launch of a Schooner
Accident to a Boy

On Saturday last, the schooner which has been built by Mr. Watson, and which has been lying on the stocks in his yard at the top of the harbour, was launched. It is about twenty years since a vessel so large has been launched from a Peel yard - the "Kate", we believe, being the last of any size - and accordingly great interest in the affair by the public.

It was expected that the vessel would be sent down the ways about twelve o'clock, and by that time crowds had assembled on the side of the Peel Hill, in the yard, and on the opposite of the river. Mrs J. Mylchreest, who had consented to perform the ceremony of the christening of the new vessel, was early on the ground, being accompanied by Mr Mylchreest, who is part owner of the vessel.

A bottle of champagne was suspended over the vessel's bow, by a blue ribbon of silk, and all impending chocks, etc., having been cleared away, Mrs Mylchreest took her stand on the platform, erected by the vessel's bow, and immediately word was given, and the vessel, clear of all restraint, slipped along the greasy ways, dashed the bottle vigorously against the vessel's stem, naming her the "Phoebe" - which name had been given in honour of Mrs. Mylchreest herself, whose Christian name it is.

Just across the river were lying some old and dismantled fishing boats, which were crowded with boys. These lads had been repeatedly warned - and, as the sequel showed, not without reason, that their position was one of danger, but they were bound to have a "front seat" at the performance, risk or no risk.

As the schooner - launched broad-side on - left the "ways," she took the water bow first, and, rolling heavily over - to the discomfiture of those on board her - slowly righted, and then bore down directly upon one of the old fishing boats - the "Victory". The boys were lined along the rail of this vessel and they made a wild rush to the shore for safety, but some were to late. The "Phoebe" crashed into her, cutting her down to the waters edge. Two lads were thrown into the water, to be immediately pulled out by those at hand, but one boy, J. Cashin, by name, and a son of Mr. W. Cashin, of Douglas, got both his hands severely jammed. Dr. McQuarrie was soon in attendance upon him, he is now doing well.

There was considerable speculation as to whether the vessel would pass under the bridge at the top of the harbour, and when a trial was made, it was found that she would not. The harbour was deepened somewhat, and everything possibly done, but to no purpose. The Harbour Board sat yesterday to consider the matter. Mr. Watson has received an order to build a 300-ton three-masted schooner.

Difficulty in Launching

A large crowd assembled at the yard on Saturday, November 18th 1892, to watch the launch of a large and handsome trawler, that had been built there for Fleetwood - the "Red Rose."

Unfortunately there was not sufficient slope in her ways, and the vessel did not move, but the launch was successfully accomplished on Monday, November 21st at noon.

The vessel was ready for sailing in a fortnight. She had beautiful lines, giving every indication of her being a fast sailer and seaworthy boat.

Yacht Launched

On Thursday, June 6th 1895, a splendid yacht was launched from Mr. Watson's yard. It was built for Mr. R. C. Howarth, of Hindley, Manchester, and there was a good crowd of visitors and residents to see the launch. Mrs. Caley, of Railway Refreshment Rooms, performed the christening.

The regulation bottle of champagne was smashed and the yacht was christened the "Martha Annie." The yacht grounded after being launched, but willing hands soon had her into deeper water, and she was soon moored in the harbour. The yacht was 50 feet over all and she was superbly finished throughout.

Dinner for Workmen

The following week on June 13th 1895, the owner of the yacht treated the workmen employed in the construction of the new yacht "Martha Annie," launched last week, to a bountiful repast.

The company that sat down to the dinner, which took place at Mrs. Caley's, Viking House, was a merry one, and numbered about 24. Justice was done to the viands provided, everyone expressing him or herself satisfied with the catering, which showed the splendid capabilities of Mrs. Caley and her staff in that direction. The only thing wanted to add to the harmony of the evening was the presence of the donor, whose absence everyone regretted.

The tables being cleared a short programme was gone through. Mr. T. Watson by the wish of the company took the chair, which was filled in a genial manner. The toast of the evening was proposed by the Chairman, "The donor of the Dinner," coupling with the name of Mr. Watson. This was enthusiastically drunk, and "For he's a jolly good fellow," was sung with gusto.

Mr. W. Watson suitably responded, trusting that the yacht would prove to be as capable as was thought, and expressing the wish that the owner might long be spared to find enjoyment in the pleasure of yachting. A song, "The Rickety-rackety crew," was then given by Mr. T. Gawne, which was much appreciated.

The next toast was "The Legislative" responded to by Mrs. S. Watson, after which Mr. C. Joughin favoured the company with a song. the toast "The Trade of Peel" was honoured, and Mr. Thomas Meyrick replied. Another song was contributed, after which the toast of "The Visitors" was proposed, Mr. Cyrus Greggor replying. This comprised the programme, and after a vote of thanks to Mr. and Mrs. Caley, the elder members of the party took their departure.

The party then settled down to a free-and-easy; speeches were given by Messrs. P. Cottier, John Teare, A. Radcliffe, Jas. Cain, etc., while songs were contributed by Messrs. Joughin, Gawne, J. Cubbon, W. Watson, H. Corris, etc., and a stump speech of unusual ability by Mr. C. Joughin. A few friends, who were thanked for their services, contributed the instrumental portion of the programme.

We might say that all of the speakers expressed their satisfaction with the general appearance of the yacht, and all agreed that the owner would be equally pleased. A remark by the chairman to the affect that all the company be invited for the trials trip was heartily agreed to. Before the company dispersed, Mrs. Caley thanked them for their kind vote of thanks. The singing of "Auld Lang Syne" terminated the evening's enjoyment.

Watson's Yard on Fire

On Sunday night of June 16th 1895, a very disastrous fire occurred in Peel resulting in the destruction of a shed and valuable contents belonging to Mr. T. Watson, shipbuilder.

The shed was situated near Kelsall's kipper yard, Mill Road, and in close proximity to the railway line. The fire was first noticed shortly after 9 o'clock. Mr A. Radcliffe, one of the fire brigade, and Mr. Sam Watson, being first to arrive on the scene. Mr. Radcliffe ran for the town fire extinguishing apparatus, and also sent a message to summon Mr. W. Kermode, captain of the Fire Brigade.

In the meantime Mr. S. Watson, with his brother and other willing helpers, ran for buckets were-ever they could procure, and returned in a very short time, when the effort was made to stem the flames, and save some of the property inside the shed.

This, however, they were unable to do, and although the Fire Brigade arrived shortly after, nothing could be done to save the building and its contents, it being one mass of flames.

The building was a wooden one, and on account of the continued dry and hot weather was easily ignited. In addition to this, it had been coated with tar, altogether making the building like tinder.

The brigade on arrival was soon at work, the hose being directed by Mr. A. Radcliffe. The water was not very voluminous, owing to the fact that the water main running along Station Road, with which it was connected, being only a two-inch one.

Willing helpers were soon at work removing spars and planks lying near the building, some of which were alight. A strong breeze blowing at the time aided the fire, and in less than half-an-hour the building was destroyed. On account of the way the wind was blowing it was feared that the fire would be communicated to Mr. Watson's premises across the river, but happily this danger was averted; a good many helpers being ready with water to put out the sparks which the wind carried across.

The shed was used for making spars, and all the contents were destroyed or rendered useless. The contents including the sails of the new yacht, which had been put there the previous day, a number of new spars, the spars of another yacht, and a large quantity of well-seasoned timber. The loss is estimated at £150, and nothing was insured. Another heavy loser, Mr. James Quayle, of Peveril Road, who used the shed as a workshop, and lost all his tools. The fire attracted a great crowd.

The cause of the fire was unknown, but it was suspected that it was caused by some lads who frequented the place to smoke and indulged in all kinds of larks. Mr. Watson left Peel by the nine o'clock train for Douglas to sail midnight for Liverpool, and as the train was going out he saw a lot of lads playing about the shed, and shouted to them to go home, a warning, which seemingly had no effect on them.

Mr. Watson was wired for to Douglas, and returned to Peel at midnight. Praise is due to the Fire Brigade for their energy and promptness, and also Inspector Boyd for the help rendered by the police force.

During 1896 shipbuilding was on the decline and the yards were only ticking over and work was mainly on repairs.

It was recorded on March 13th 1897, that two nobbys were being built at Mr. Watson's yard and would be ready for the mid season herring season and these were duly launched as announced.

With the decline of the fishing there was also a decline in shipbuilding and the number of yards had also dwindled, even Graves yard had closed, leaving only two shipyards in Peel. One was the new firm of Neakle and Watterson, who had taken over Graves yard on the quay, and Watson's. However, both firms managed to keep going pretty well for a while, and in 1898 were turning out a boat on average every seven to ten weeks.

Four launchings were recorded at Watson's yard, one of which was for England, two for the Irish fishery, and one for Peel.

The first was in March 1898, it being a yacht for a Lancashire man. It was named "Edith Annie" being a forty tonner, 63 feet in length, with a 14 feet beam. The internal arrangements were planned for comfort, comprising of saloon, stateroom, ladies cabin, pantry, etc., and most of the fittings were in teak. The vessel was ketch rigged as it was the handiest and most easily worked. It was intended for cruising.

The second vessel was launched in September, 1898, it being a nobby "Amethyst" which was 37 feet overall and with a 30 feet keel and 12 feet beam. It was for the Galway fishing and took nine weeks to build.

Two nobbys were launched on the same day in January 1899. The first was named the "St. Peter" and was for the Galway fishing. 38 feet overall and had a beam of 11 feet 6 inches.

The other was named "Bluebell" and was for Mr. Phipps, of Peel. The measurements were the same as "St. Peter."

During the next few years there were very few boats built and the yards depended on a great deal of repairs.

Then on September 17th 1904 it was recorded that the keel of a large trawler for Fleetwood had been laid down at the yard of Mr. T. Watson, and work was being pushed along with all possible despatch. The owner was in Peel the previous week in one of his trawlers giving final instructions for his new vessel. He has had a most successful career in the fishing industry, proving that there is still money to be made out of it.

However, by 1908 Mr. Watson had gone into financial difficulties and the firm went into liquidation and eventually Mr. Watson had to live with one of his sons who had previously emigrated to Canada. Although Peel could still claim to have one good shipbuilder, the closure of this yard virtually ended that great era of shipbuilding in Peel which started almost 60 years before, and almost an era of a man had contributed so much by building a wide variety of ships for all purposes and of varying sizes and it was a pity that it had to end the way it did.

Chapter Seven

Neakle & Watterson's Shipyard
The End of a Great Era

It was in 1897 that saw the creation of a shipbuilding firm that saw the end of the great era of shipbuilding in Peel, and also changed with the times, building a wide range of vessels including fast sailing yachts, fishing boats for sailing, motor fishing boats, steam drifters, and iron keeled vessels.

The firm started under the title of Messrs. Neakle, Watterson and Cashen, and later they set up in business when the Graves yard closed earlier that year, operating from the same yard on the quay between the coal yard and the Viking Longhouse. They operated very successfully for over thirty years, and changed the site of the yard to more suitable surroundings on the Mill Road close to the old mill in 1907. Then later moved across the river to the site that in more recent times was occupied by West Marine.

The first reference to the business was on March 13th 1897, and was as follows - "The new firm of Messrs. Neakle Watterson and Cashen, who had taken over Graves yard, had on March 10th 1897, launched a fishing boat. It was named "Minnie" and was built to the order of Mr. A. H. Bailey, Castle Street, Peel. The vessel is 27'/₂ feet long with a 10 feet beam, and will proceed to the south of Ireland fishery."

Then on January 1st 1898, it was recorded - "The splendid nobby just built by Messrs. Neakle, Watterson and Cashen, for the Dublin Castle Congested Board, was successfully launched on Monday morning. She was taken on a carriage along the quay from the shipyard and launched down the slipway near the Railway Station. There were plenty of willing helpers, and the actual launching was accomplished in a smart manner. The nobby was named "Morning Star," and will be immediately rigged and fitted out, and sent to her destination on the west of Ireland. The craft is trim and serviceable looking and will do credit to the good name for boat building borne by Peel. This firm has also secured an order for a second nobby for the Dublin Congested Board, of which Mr. T. Shimmin, of Peel, is the representative. The nobbys fishing in Galway Bay have done extremely well in the late fishing, and the board are continually adding new boats to their already large and well-fitted stock of nobbys.

They have a repeat order and the keel of the new boat will be laid at once.

Launch of a Fishing Boat

The following was published on April 2nd 1893 - "Last Wednesday week there was launched from Mr. Graves' yard, the quay, a fishing nobby built by Messrs. Neakle, Wattson and Cashen. She is 26'/₂ feet long, and 10'/₂ feet beam, and is called the "Ruby." She is built to the order of "The Dublin Castle Congested Board," and will hail from Clifton, Galway. A Peel man (Mr. R. Quilliam), is to be given the command. He has also been commissioned by the Board to instruct the inhabitants of Galway Coast in fishing of all descriptions. Early in the New Year, a similar craft, was built by the same firm for the "Dublin Castle Congested Districts Board." The vessel is under the command of another Peel man (Mr. J. Crellin), who is employed in the same capacity as Mr. Quilliam, that is, instructing Galway crofters in the art of fishing. Last summer the Galway boats had a very successful herring fishery, some of the vessels earning as much as £300 each. The "Ruby," is of a very handsome and useful build, and the builders are gaining a well-merited name for trim and seaworthy vessels. The fact they have obtained a second order from the Dublin Castle Board speaks volumes for the excellence of their workmanship.

The following was revealed on September 17th 1898 - "Another large nobby was launched on Saturday, from Messrs. Neakle and Watterson's yard on the quay. Built to the order of the Dublin Castle Congested Districts Board, and will hail from Clifden, Co. Galway. She is numbered 712D, and has been named "St. Joseph". They are doing a splendid work in assisting the fishermen on the western Irish coast and the Manx Government might very well undertake similar work to theirs. The Peel fishermen have practically no incentive to take an interest in the fishing under the prevailing conditions, which, were the Government to assist them in the manner of the Irish authorities, might land a new lease of life into a decaying industry. The "St. Joseph" is a large nobby of 30 feet keel, and 11 feet beam. She has been altogether about ten weeks in hand. She is the third nobby launched this year by this firm by the Board, which is ample proof of the satisfactory build of their boats. She is a very pretty model, and will give satisfaction both as a fair and foul weather boat. As soon as the nobby is completed Messrs. T. Moughtin and J. Wilson will navigate her to Ireland.

While in February 1899, another nobby was launched for the Galway fishing. She was the "Connemara Lass" being 46 feet overall, with a keel of 36 feet and a beam of 13 feet, and had a displacement of $20^{1}/_{2}$ tons. There was a large cabin aft with sleeping accommodation for eight men.

It was recorded on June 24th, 1899 - "A nobby for Mr. John Jenkins, to sail under the name of "El Dorado," was launched from

Messrs. Neakle and Watterson's yard on Saturday week. She is a neat looking craft, and an acquisition to the local fleet. Her measurements are 40 feet overall, and a 11'/₂ beam. This firm has received an order from the Congested Districts Board for a nobby on the lines of one recently built by them for the Board.

Then on Saturday, September 9th, 1899, The "Maria," a nobby was launched.

There appeared to be a quiet spell during the early part of 1900 as the only launch referred to was on October 27th 1900, when a 30-foot nobby was launched for Mr. Healy, of Cashircaveen, called the "Saint Attracta."

Further news was revealed on March 23rd. 1901, the item being "A satisfactory launch took place at Neakle and Watterson's yard, quay, on Thursday morning - a 36 foot nobby built for the Dublin Castle Congested Districts Board. She will be named "Evening Star," and will hail from Roundstone, Galway. The vessel glided easily into the water.

They have two orders still on their books - a yacht for a Glasgow gentleman, and a fishing boat for a local owner.

Next came a report of August 10th 1901.

Launch of a Yacht

On Monday there was successfully launched from Messrs. Neakle and Watterson's yard, on Peel Quay, a trim looking 21-ton cruising yacht for Mr. Harold D. Jackson, of Glasgow, son of Mrs. Stewart-Jackson, of Thie Jairg, Peel, and a grandson of ex-Deemster Sir W. L. Drinkwater.

Mr Jackson intends to use his neat little vessel on the Clyde. She will be named the "Bride" and measures 44 feet over-all. All the fittings will be of a first class kind. It is encouraging to the Peel fishing industry for local builders to have the opportunity of turning out craft like Mr. Jackson's, and judging by appearance he will possess a trustworthy vessel.

Serious Accident
A Man Hurt

A double accident having a serious and a comic side occurred at the launch. The builders had to have the quay specially dug up to allow the vessel being launched from the yard into the harbour, and blocking the traffic by the "ways," was a great source of curiosity to the visitors in the town during the day.

At the appointed time for the launch there was a huge crowd of spectators, whose crushing was a great inconvenience to the men assisting at the launch. Even the presence of two policemen was insufficient to lessen the pressure of the crowd.

After being freed, the yacht moved down the "ways" and then became fast through one of the holding chains having broken. The matter remedied she then "took" to the water with considerable force. The "Bride" had a passenger on board in the person of Mr. John Rawlinson, formerly of Peel, and as the vessel went over the end of the "ways" he was pitched head foremost into the water. He re-appeared almost instantly with pipe he had been previously smoking still in his mouth, causing great laughter amongst the spectators.

Being a good swimmer he was soon safely on "terra-firma." Meanwhile, a further calamity had occurred, Mr. Henry Cowley, skipper of Mr. Howarth's yacht, the "Edith Annie," was standing near the "ways," and as the vessel entered the water a beam upended, hitting him with considerable force on the stomach and legs. His condition was such that a medical man was called in, and Dr. Kelman, after examining the injured man, ordered him to Noble's Hospital, whence he was transferred shortly afterwards. Mr. Cowley is said to be progressing towards recovery.

While on August 31st. 1901 the following was published - " We regret to state that Mr. Henry Cowley who was injured at the launch of the yacht on Bank Holiday Monday, and who has been in Noble's Hospital ever since, had his leg amputated above the knee on Saturday.

Mr. Cowley did recover but spent the rest of his life on crutches.

The next news was published on February 15th 1902 - "On Monday a thirty-foot nobby, not yet named, was launched from Messrs. Neakle and Watterson's yard, on the quay, the vessel, which is a neat useful one, taking the water with ease."

Another launch was recorded on June 17th 1902 - "On Saturday a thirty ton yawl-rigged yacht name "Ada", built to the order of Mr. Hodder, of Queenstown. There was a large crowd present at the launch, which was effected with despatch. The vessel buillt to plans of Messrs. Neakle and Watterson's own, and looks graceful and speedy. They have several other orders on hand. At the present they have two others yachts laid down, one for a Ramsey owner, Major Banaster, and the other, a small one, for Caesar Cashin, of Peel."

A report on July 12th. 1902 stated - "The yacht built by Messrs. Neakle and Watterson sailed on Saturday evening from Peel, with her owner, Captain F. Hodder, of Ballea Castle, Caraline, Queenstown, and his wife on board. The yacht "Ada" is yawl-rigged and is 35 tons. Though intended as a racer, she has excellent accommodation for guests and crew. There is a ladies cabin, and owner's state room, with commodious saloon, and altogether a very comfortable boat. The yacht sails were designed and made by Mr. W. E. Teare, and were perfect examples of the art of sailmaking."

"On Tuesday evening the following telegram was received by Messrs. Neakle and Watterson from Captain Hodder - "Came in here (Dunmore) from heavy weather. Yacht behaved splendidly. Delighted with her."

The next item appeared on July 26th 1902, it being

A Peel Built Crack Yacht

The following, very satisfactory, letter has been received by Messrs. Neakle and Watterson, who will feel gratified that their handcraftsmanship has turned out so well.

I have much pleasure in expressing the greatest satisfaction with the yacht. We had her in all sorts of weather from calf's to gales, and I find her going along in light weather, and also fast and powerful in strong wind and sea. I find her handy as a five tonner. This morning I beat her up to the anchorage here, which is a very narrow channel, and although the wind was very light and she only had about twice her own length to turn in, she came up like an 18 foot boat. I also have pleasure in stating that everything on board her, aloft, on deck, and below, has worked perfectly without the slightest hitch. Everyone who has seen her up to the present has admired her immensely. All the people in Dunmore said she was the handsomest yacht that has ever been in there - Wishing you future success, I remain, yours faithfully, FRANCIS J. HODDER.

Then on September 6th 1902 - "a smack was successfully launched from this firm on Thursday, for a Ramsey owner."

While on October 11th 1902 it was reported - "The cutter" Emerald Bay" built by Messrs. Neakle and Watterson, of Peel, to the order of Major Banaster, of Ramsey, had a trial trip in the Bay on Monday, when the next little vessel performed excellently. She was a shapely craft, and will do credit to her builders.

While on October 18th 1902, the following article was published about the new vessel -

Praise for "Emerald Ray"

The maritime correspondent of the "Ramsey Courier" had subjected the new addition to the Ramsey fleet of crack boats - the

"Emerald Ray," recently built to Major Banaster's orders by Messrs. Neakle and Watterson, of Peel - to keen criticism, and the result is complimentary to the young firm of boat builders. He say's "that the "Emerald Ray" is in advance of everything in her class owned in Ramsey, and congratulates both designers and builders upon the happy result arrived at, and hopes the Major may never have the slightest cause to regret the day that he went in for home industry. " On Saturday last, the "Emerald Ray" had her trial with another crack boat - the "Defender" - also belonging to Major Banaster. Notwithstanding the crew were new to the boat, and the sails found to be of not quite perfect fit, the "Emerald Ray" finished close up to the "Defenders" stern. The Defender is perhaps the smartest boat of her class in the Island. Another trial was given to the yacht on Tuesday morning, in a stiff breeze, which evidently suited the boat's capacity.

The next year also proved to be a busy year. The first reference came on February 7th. 1903 - "A cutter yacht for a Douglas owner was successfully launched from Messrs. Neakle and Watterson's yard on Saturday.

A continuation of this story was published on February 14th 1903 - "The cutter yacht "Kathleen" for Mr. Moore, of Douglas has been fitted and put to sea on Wednesday to engage temporarily in the long-line fishing. The owner intends to bring her round to Douglas, where she will follow the long-line fishing, until summer, when she will be used as a yacht. The measurements of the vessel are - 47 feet over-all, 29 feet keel and beam 12^1/$_2$ feet.

The next episode about this boat was reported on February 21st 1903 - " The Kathleen now fishing off Douglas. Her passage round to the East was done in record time -- especially through the Sound and up by Langness. The trim little vessel is winning praise from everybody."

The saying that the Peel built boats were the fastest ships afloat seemed to be reflected in the following, which was published on June 27th 1903 -

Success of Peel Built Yachts at Douglas

"The regatta at Douglas was chiefly interesting to Peel folk by the reason of two of the competitors in the race for the open or half decked licensed boats being Peel built. The "Kathleen" (W. Moore), Douglas, and "Emerald Ray" (Major Banaster), Ramsey, both built by Messrs. Neakle and Watterson, of Peel, were respectively first and second."

Another tribute to the firm's skill was published on May 23rd 1903 - "Peel has ever been noted for its shipbuilding - the Peel built smacks of the middle of the century having a world wide fame. In view of the decline of the fishing industry, Messrs. Neakle and Watterson are making a speciality of yacht building, and at present have two small craft on the stocks, one 34-foot racer for Messrs. King and Porter, of Liverpool, and 32 footer for Mr. John Wilson, of Peel. In addition they are overhauling a schooner-yacht "Bedouin," belonging to Colonel Moore, Great Meadow."

An outline of the launch and details of the yacht were published on July 4th 1903 -

Launch of a Yacht

On Tuesday was launched, the yacht Messrs. Neakle and Watterson are building to the order of Messrs. Porter and King, of the Royal Mersey Yacht Club. The yacht, which is named "Lilian," is 34 feet over all and 8 feet beam, and will be cutter rigged. She is of the modern racer build, and is meant for cruising as well as for racing, having both forecastle and saloon accommodation.

The "Lilian" is expected to sail for Liverpool today (Saturday), and she will take part in the club races on July 11th.

The story continued on July 11th with the following - "The Lilian - the race yacht launched last week by Messrs. Neakle and Watterson left Peel on Saturday for the Mersey, but was driven back early on Sunday by a north-west gale. A successful crossing of the Irish Sea, was however, made on Wednesday in comparative calm weather, Messrs. Callister and Quirk were the navigators. The little craft departed from Peel on Tuesday evening but was becalmed at Port Erin and had to be rowed through the sound. A giant breeze blew up early on Wednesday morning, and the 79 miles between the Calf and New Brighton were covered within 10 hours - a very satisfactory speed."

The vessel's first success was recorded on July 15th 1903 - "Word was received from Messrs. King and Porter, the owners, by Messrs. Neakle and Watterson, that the yacht "Lilian," recently launched from their yard, had won in a race on Saturday by nine minutes."

A further launch was recorded on July 15th. 1903 - "A cutter yacht measuring 32 feet 8 inches, and named "Constance" built to the order of Mr. John Wilson, of Peel, was launched from Messrs. Neakle and Watterson's yard on Wednesday. She is on the lines of the "Lilian."

There appeared to be a slight lull in the trade then, as was revealed on October 3rd 1903 - "The lull in the yacht building trade of Peel has come to an end by Messrs. Neakle and Watterson receiving an order a forty ton racing cruiser for a Southport owner, to be finished in March next. The vessel will be on the lines of the yacht built and launched that year to the order of Mr. Hodder, of Queenstown, which gave such unbounded satisfaction.

The on November 7th 1903, more details of the yacht were published - "Messrs. Neakle and Watterson are at present at work on a 40 ton yacht, being built to the order of Mr. Rowe, of Southport, which will be the largest vessel of its class built in Peel. The order for the iron keel was placed with Mr. J. Clague and Son, Ramsey, and it is noteworthy as it is the largest casting the firm has ever undertaken.

The keel of the "rocker" type, measures about 25 feet in length, and has a total weight of 5½ tons. It is cast in three pieces, the centre block, which is heaviest, weighing 2½ tons. The keel partakes of the shape of the yacht, and deep slots and tongues are provided for connecting the pieces.

While on December 12th 1903 it was reported that the firm had received an order from a Dingle owner.

The launch was the next reference recorded it being March 5th 1904 as follows - "A large and interested crowd watched to launch on Thursday morning of a 40 ton racing yacht for Mr. Rowe, of Southport, owner of the yacht "Dorothy," which is a frequent visitor to Peel. The "ways" were fixed across the roadway from the yard, and the vessel glided into the water in the smoothest possible manner promptly at 11.45 a.m. The owner was present at the launch and was first to board the yacht after she entered the water. The yacht is a very shapely and beautiful model and a credit to her Peel draughtsmen."

A further report on March 12th 1904 revealed - "Messrs. Neakle and Watterson's latest production - the forty ton fast cruising yacht launched on Thursday week for T. B. Rowe, Esq., of Southport - is to be ready for sailing at Easter. Mr. Rowe, who is immensely pleased with his new craft, has decided to name her like his former yacht, "Dorothy." Messrs. John Clague and Son Limited, of Ramsey, cast the iron keel of the vessel, and ways six tons. The "Dorothy's" length over all is 61 feet. There will be three cabins - the main saloon, ladies saloon, and crew's cabin - the fittings of which are to be pitch pine and teak, while the sanitary fittings are up-to-date. The vessel will be yawl rigged and Mr W. E. Teare is designing and making the sails. Altogether the "Dorothy" will be a yacht of which Peel can be well proud.

This firm of boat-builders have also half-a-dozen orders on their books - enough work to keep a large staff busily engaged until midsummer. Four of them are "nobbys," two for Dingle owners, and two for local men - one each for Messrs. Killey and Gaskell. Mr. John Wilson has ordered a yacht, and also has Mr. Jas. Cregeen, of Port Erin. Both the latter are required in time for the visitors."

The next report concerned a launch on June 4th 1904 - "A nobby of rather larger dimentions than usual - 34 foot keel was launched from Messrs. Neakle and Watterson's yard on Monday in the presence of a numerous crowd. The craft is trimly built as all this progressive firms productions are, and the launch was in every way successful. The owner is Mr. John Killey, of Peel, formerly of the lugger "Jane."

While on June 12th 1904 more details of the success of the "Lilian" were revealed - "The racing yacht "Lilian," built in Peel last year for Messrs. Porter and King is doing excellent sailing for her owners. On Saturday week she won a handicap sailing in the Mersey, organised by the Tranmere Sailing Club, and in the Royal Mersey Regatta, this week, the "Lilian" won again, beating a new crack Arnside boat. The "Lilian" bears the great honour of not yet having been beaten."

Then in early July a nobby for the Congested District Board was launched from Messrs. Neakle and Watterson's yard. This was followed by a report on July 30th. 1904 - "The new nobby, recently launched, left for Dingle, to which port she will be attached, on Monday morning."

A sign that the firm was still keeping busy was revealed in a report dated September 3rd 1904 - "Another cargo of timber has been discharged during the week - this time from the "Bessie" for Messrs. Neakle and Watterson, shipbuilders."

While on September 17th 1904 it was reported that this shipyard has had a very busy year, and on Saturday launched a 32-foot nobby for the Congested Districts Board, Dublin Castle, Ireland. This vessel is a neat compact model, and is a worthy product of this firm's workmanship. It has been named the "Majestic" and will be sailed across to the Emerald Isle in the course of a few days some of the Board's men having arrived to take charge. The firm having laid down the keel of another large nobby. This vessel was duly completed and launched, fitted, and sailed for her home port of Dingle. She was named "St. Michael."

The firm still continued to hold their own as shown in the following published on April 1st. 1905 - "Messrs. Neakle and Watterson have been busily engaged for some time on a 36 foot nobby for a Baltimore fishing boat owner, and it was successfully launched on Wednesday. It has not yet been named, as the owner intends doing that when he comes to Peel this week. He has great faith in Peel shipbuilding, a faith, which judging by the shapely new vessel, is well placed."

The firm were also improving their equipment as revealed on June 3rd 1905 - "Messrs. Neakle and Watterson are busy laying down a large new gas engine for wood sawing purposes.

Very Fast Boats

How good and speedy the firm's boats were, was disclosed in the same paper - "A telegram has been received by them from Mr. Porter, owner of the cutter "Lilian" (built by them) stating that the yacht had won the Ailsa Cup last week, adding that she has not yet been beaten."

The next reference was on October 14th 1905 - "Messrs. Neakle and Watterson, have their staff busily engaged on a 25 ton cruising yacht for Mr. C. F. Egner, a well known Peel visitor."

Yacht Launched in Peel

Details of the launch of this yacht were given on April 14th 1906 - "A launch ever attracts large crowds in a seafaring community like ours. It is not surprising therefore that on Wednesday last, in magnificent weather, a very large crowd should gather on the quay to watch the launch of a 25 ton fast cruising yacht, built by Messrs. Neakle and Watterson to the order of Mr. C. F. Egner, of Ballaquane. The yacht, during construction, has been generally admired for her graceful lines, and it undoubtedly is a cleverly designed and beautiful creation. The time fixed for the launch was noon, and the yacht sped down the ways and into the water in the easiest manner possible. Mr. Egner has selected the name "Dolores" for his new possession. She will be fitted with every modern adjunct to comfortable handling.

Even to variest amateur cannot but be struck with the elegant lines of the new yacht. Build and rig have been designed in accordance with the latest ideas, but comfort has not been lost sight of, while the superfine materials and fittings used to make the "Dolores" the daintiest production by far of anything yet turned out in the yacht line by this firm.

The deck is laid in best American pine, with the centrepieces in lights of teak. The steering pit is also fitted with teak. Chaste brass work increases the finished appearance of the deck. On the rudder is inscribed "Dolores," with the names of the builders.

Below is a veritable wonderland of compactness and luxury. The principle cabin abaft the forecastle is fitted with polished teak and furnished in crimson plush. There is ample seating accommodation, a most ingenious weighted swinging table (always level irrespective of the vessel rolling), marvellous sets of drawers (they exist in every imaginable corner), and every accessory to comfort.

The ladies' cabin, sternwise of the main cabin, is, if possible, more luxurious of the other. Also of polished teak, it is most prettily furnished in green plush, with mirror and lavatory at one end. The lights are neatly curtained, and the sleeping berths can only be characterised as princely. Lockers for clothing and sundry other comfort aids, make the apartment such, that any lady could live here for a month with little desires for terra firma. In evidence of the completeness of the furnishing, even the candle holders are of polished brass, with a handy arrangement for allowing the candle to move upwards as it is in the process of burning.

The sailors are housed in the forecastle very comfortably, and there is room for three. Another marvel of the multum is parvo the combined lavatory and w.c. The washbasin closes against the side of the ship, and after using, the wastewater automatically runs to the w.c. basin, where it can be pumped away.

Taken in toto, the "Dolores," is a beautiful piece of handcraftsmanship. Mr. G. H. Kermode supplied the upholstery, and Mr. J. Cannell has been responsible for the plumbing. Both sub-departments have been carried out in the best manner.

Trials

It was reported on July 3rd 1906 that Mr. Egner's new yacht, the "Dolores," was brought out for a trial trip on Monday, and in a splendid fitting suit of sails (made by Messrs. Teare and Sons), sailed to the entire satisfaction of the owners and builders. The yawl of a yacht, which is the neat handcraftsmanship of Mr. Wm. Lace, Glenfaba Road. This little boat is entirely in keeping with the yacht, has a drop-keel and is fitted so that a mast can be used if necessary.

During this period the firm disposed of their nobby "Bee" and are building another in place of the one they sold. They are also busy transforming the old nickey "Telegraph" into a trawler, for a Dingle owner. They have performed their work in good style, and the vessel looks neater, stronger, and more seaworthy than ever. The owner has named the trawler "St. Ita."

After this the firm built and launched a fishing boat and then they fitted her. Details of the departure of this vessel were published on November 24th 1906 - " On Saturday last, a nobby for the Dublin Castle Congested districts Board. The new vessel, which is of 34 keel, and is named "Star of the Sea," will sail out of Sligo. A Sligo crew will sail the vessel to her home port under the charge of Mr. W. Jones, of Peel."

Then on March 9th 1907, the following report appeared - "The iron-keel - about 3 tons weight - for the half-decker which is being built for a Ramsey owner was cast at Messrs. J. Clague and Sons ironworks, Ramsey, last week. The new creation is to be up-to-date in every respect, and is expected to be ready in time for next summer's yachting.

This vessel was duly completed, launched and fitted and reference was made to its departure on July 27th 1907 - "The half-decker for the northern port left on Saturday trim and complete. The dead calm made the voyage round the Point of Ayre nearly a 24 hour one. On Sunday the new craft, lying at the quay at Ramsey was the cynosure of all eyes. The new boat is called "Ben Varrey" - meaning "girl of the sea" or "Mermaid."

Moved their Yard

On May 18th 1907 reference was made to the firm moving their yard from the quay to Mill Road where Mr. T. Watson has part of his yard, the other part being on the other side of the river. The area referred to was that now occupied by N.R.Corlett Ltd. and the Peel Town Commissioners' Yard and this area had been newly enclosed for them.

It is also referred to them laying the keel of a large drifter, which they were building for Mr. C. F. Egner. Work progressed on this vessel until in April 4th 1908, the following report appeared -

Launch of Peel's First Herring Drifter

Thursday, April 2nd 1908, will go down to posterity as an important date in the annals of Peel - the launch of the first Manx steam herring drifter, Mr. C. F. Egner's "Manx Princess," PL29.

The unfortunate decline of the sail fishing industry to its present condition, has directed attention to any possible means of bring back the smile of prosperity once more to our ancient fishing centre, and while suggestions have been made for many years to build "drifters," it has remained for a progressive English gentleman resident in Peel, Mr C. F. Egner, who has shown his practical interest in several directions, to take the initiative in the matter by placing and order with Messrs. Neakle and Watterson to lay down the keel of one of these vessels.

It is to the credit of this enterprising firm that, though they had not the slightest acquaintance with drifted building, they accepted the order, and wholly designed the drifter and have carried it to its completion so excellently that it is not too much to predict that they not be short of similar commissions in the future.

The new vessel has just occupied six months in her building, work being commenced at the end of the summer, so that she has been expeditiously turned out. When the news of the order being given was first known it was received with almost jubilation by those interested in the fishing industry, and it is fondly hoped that if the vessel is successful it will mean the turning point in the fortunes of the Peel Fishing.

Thursday was the ideal day for the auspicious occasion - fine and spring like - and the sun shone out brilliantly at the hour fixed for the launch - half past eleven. Several hundreds of interested spectators gathered in the vicinity - the side of Peel Hill overlooking the shipbuilders' yard at Peel Hill, being the venue for a considerable crowd.

The builders had gone to extreme care in fixing ways, everything possibly being done to ensure a successful send-off. On a platform erected near the bow of the drifter, Mr. Egner stood in company of Miss. Evelyn Christian, third daughter of Mr. E. T. Christian, who was honoured by being chosen to perform the ceremony.

As the vessel commenced to move down the ways, Miss Christian dashed the bottle of champagne, which was suspended by a blue ribbon upon the vessel, and, naming the drifter the "Manx Princess," wished every success and prosperity. The vessel slid quickly down the ways, entering the water cleanly and neatly - in fact, the launch being everything that could be desired.

The dimensions of the "Manx Princess" are - length 100 feet; beam 19 feet; depth 10 feet. She will be fitted with engines of 250-horse power, and which will develop a speed of over 11 knots. The framework of the vessel is of extremely strong kind, and the engines highest grade, and of the most up-to-date make. She will be lit throughout with acetylene gas. The outfit of nets is being supplied by the Gourock Ropework Company.

The Glasgow engineers who are fitting in the machinery have had some men in Peel putting in the various parts, including the stern tube, tail shaft, sea cocks, and propeller, so that when the vessel will be towed to Govan in a week or two everything will be in position, to enable the "Manx Princess" to be finally completed with as little delay as possible.

The drifter will be under the command of Mr F. Corris, of Church Street, Peel, who is one of the most experienced captains in Peel, and will carry a crew of ten.

It is intended to fish her in the first instance off the East Coast of England and Scotland.

After initial fittings were placed in her she was towed to Scotland for her engine to be fitted. Then it was reported - "On Saturday June 8th 1908, Mr. Egners new steam drifter, "Manx Princess," is a workman- like and thoroughly finished vessel, and one which should make a good record for herself.

Abaft are the sleeping quarters for the men, the eight bunks being models of neatness. They are screened off by curtains on brass rails, and the place is lit by acetylene and adequately heated; adjoining this is the galley and further forward the engines.

These have been constructed by one of the best known and reputable firms in the trade - Messrs. McKee and Baxter, of Copland Works, Govan, Glasgow, and are of the compound, inverted, direct-acting, surface condensing type. They are the very latest and third pattern for steam drifter work, their speciality being to give maximum speed with minimum of coal consumption.

Between the engine and the forecastle is the section of the ship dealing with the herring. The bulk of the fish go down through the deck opening into boxes at the sides, those remaining in the nets falling through the griddled platform, to be picked out beneath.

In the forecastle there is a further section for sleeping accommodation and storage for various purposes.

Spick and span from bow to stern, the "Manx Princess," PL29, bade goodbye to Peel on Wednesday, July 19th 1908, en-route for the Shetland fishing ground. The men are all Peelites - F. Corris (master), W. Cain (mate), A. Cowley (engineer), P. Teare (fireman), C. Cashen, E. Moore, J. Cain, J. Cowell, and L. Greggor crew.

During the period that the drifter was being built, preparatory work for the building of other vessels was in progress. It was revealed on March 14th 1908 - "The iron keel for Mr. J. Clarey's new half decker which is shortly to be built by Messrs. Neakle and Watterson was cast at Messrs. John Clague and Sons foundry, Ramsey, last week. The casting is about three tons weight. As soon as the new drifter is out of their hands, they will commence a nobby for Mr. Robert Gell, Circular Road, the keel of which has just been cast in Birkenhead.

The announcement for the launch of the nobby was made on July 18th 1908 - "On Tuesday morning the firm launched a 30 foot nobby for Mr. Robert Gell - a shapely and up-to-date little vessel. Like

Mr. Gell's former nobby, she is to be named "Cushag," and has been registered under the Board of Trade."

The next launch was reported on August 22nd 1908 - "On Wednesday of last week Messrs. Neakle and Watterson launched from their new yard at Peel Mill, a half decker for Mr. Rowan, of Liverpool, and which is to be sailed from Ramsey under Skipper J. Clarrey. The vessel looks neat and speedy, and may be expected to give a good account of itself. The keels of two more vessels have been laid in the yard.

A tribute to the workmanship of this yard is reflected in the following, which was published on August 29th 1908 -

The Latest Half-Decker Built at Peel

The maritime correspondent of the "Ramsey Courier" writes in the following strain regarding the latest vessel launched by this firm of shipbuilders: - "The newest half-decker cutter-yacht "Caribou" arrived here from Peel on Sunday, in charge of Skipper John Clarey. She is the latest creation of Messrs. Neakle and Watterson, of Peel, and is built to the order of Mr. W. J. Rowan, of Liverpool, for Skipper John Clarey, and will be used for yachting in the summer and fishing in the winter.

The "Caribou" is 46 feet and 6 inches over all, 35 feet odd on the water line, 13-foot beam outside and draws about 5 feet 9 inches. She has the orthodox cut away bow, raked sternpost, and hollow bottom. In fact many features, the new boat resembles the "Ben Varrey," "Marguerite," and others by the same builder.

Whether she will show a great turn of speed remains to be seen; but one other thing is certain, and it is the fact that from her ample beam and broad bilges she is bound to possess great canvas-carrying powers and stability, and these are features closely allied to speed. It is not the craft that stands up to her canvas that makes the best speed, especially to the windward? As a rule it is, because when the stiff ship is pressed she adds to her draft, whereas, under similar circumstances the craft through careening over, lessens her draught of the water, and consequently blows away to leeward. However, be this as it may, judging by her lines, it seems safe to predict that "Caribou" will give a very good account of herself. She is strong as a rock, is nicely fitted below with every convenience for cruising purposes, and will make a grand craft for fishing. In short the "Caribou" is altogether a fine specimen of the up-to-date half-decker, and is such she has past her muster among the Ramsey "experts." And I think Mr. Rowan and skipper Clarey have every reason to be proud of their new craft.

The next report was on October 24th 1908 - "in the best weather on Tuesday week, Messrs. Neakle and Watterson launched from their yard at Peel Mill, a fishing nobby for Mr. John Devine, of Dingle, Ireland. The launch was in every way successful. The new nobby is of 30 foot keel, and measures 44 feet overall. She is one of great many similar vessels built by the same enterprising firm for Ireland.

A second nobby to the order of a Valentia owner is just approaching completion.

A very special complement has just been paid to these builders. The Govan firm of engineers who fitted the engines to Mr. Egner's steam drifter, the "Manx Princess," in the spring of this year, has asked Messrs. Neakle and Watterson, in view of the pleasing fact that the "Manx Princess" sails much faster that other similar vessels fitted with the same make of engines, to forward details of her design.

It is the intention of the Scotish firm to turn out five steam drifters, and they offered Messrs. Neakle and Watterson the building of one. The members of the firm have reason to feel proud of this tribute to the excellence of their work."

Business was brisk as was revealed on October 31st 1908 - "Two launches of fishing boats, both for the Emerald Isle, have taken place this week. On Tuesday Messrs. Neakle and Watterson from their yard, Peel Mill, launched a 45 feet overall nobby for Mr. M. O'Connell, of Bigness Island, Valentia. This vessel has an iron keel, weighing a ton, and has the firm's usual care and excellent workmanship bestowed upon it. The launch was highly successful in every respect.

The other launch was at Watson's yard across the river

Moving to February 20th 1909 - " On Tuesday morning there was launched from the yard of Messrs. Neakle and Watterson, Peel Mill, a half-decker for Mr. Lawson, of Laxey - a little vessel which is reckoned by those best able to know, as one of the smartest models yet built in Peel, and one we feel sure which from her graceful lines will show herself amongst the speediest of her kind on the Island. She will be used for fishing in the winter and yachting in the summer. Her measurements are 42 feet overall, and 12 feet beam. There is $2^1/_2$ tons of iron in her keel, and everything on board is in keeping with the reputation of the firm for reliable work.

The next mention was on April 24th 1909 - "On Wednesday morning Messrs. Neakle and Watterson launched from their Peel Mill Yard, a nobby, ordered though the Dublin Castle Congested Districts Board for a Dingle proprietor. She is a particularly trim model, and has been built with the care and excellence for which the firm are achieving a name. The launch was accomplished with facility, the boat sliding sideways from the yard into the river with ease. As there was a high tide at that time, this very much-helped matters. The measurements of the new nobby are 31 feet keel, and 13 feet beam. Another nobby for Ireland is rapidly approaching completion in the same firm's yard.

While on May 29th 1909 there appeared - "A particularly excellent launch was made from Messrs. Neakle and Watterson's yard, Peel Mill, on Saturday - a 46 foot over-all nobby for Mr. D.

Graham, of Dingle, County Kerry, Ireland. A new vessel is an admirable specimen of the firm's workmanship is worthy to note that this is the third family, which have patronised the builders. Unfortunately the completion of the nobby finishes the orders of Messrs. Neakle and Watterson have on their books. For the sake of providing work, it is sincerely hoped that orders will soon flow again.

The next reference was good news, which was on September 25th 1909 as follows -

Another New Steam Drifter
Mr. Egners Enterprise

Mr. C. F. Egners is again displaying his great enterprise, and his consideration for Peel, in having ordered a second steam drifter, to be built in the yard of Messrs. Neakle and Watterson, Peel Mill. This is an undoubted proof that his venture in building the "Manx Princess" has been a success, in fact her net earnings at Lerwick this year have been very encouraging, despite a rather poor season. The new drifter, we are informed by Mr. Egner, is to be somewhat smaller than his last, and she is to be completed by the 1st June next year. Her first trial will be in home waters - at the herring fishing next season. She is to be fitted out for line fishing for the winter of 1910/11, after the herring fishing will be concluded. The building of the new drifter will provide needed work for artisans, who have been experiencing a slack time of late.

On November 30th 1909 it was reported that the keel of Mr. Egner's new steam drifter had been laid that week.

Work on this vessel proceeded at a good pace and then on April 16th 1910 came the following article.

Launch of Mr. Egner's Second Drifter

In view of the pleasing fact that Mr. C. F. Egner's first steam drifter, the "Manx Princess," has been a financial success, and in the hope that these vessels may mean the restoration of Peel's prosperity, vast interest has been displayed in the following yard of Messrs. Neakle and Watterson, of a second drifter for Mr. Egner.

The latest production of the builders was only laid down in November last, and considering the frigidity and storminess of the weather during the past winter, which is a serious deterrent to outdoor work, everybody concerned should be congratulated on the speed with which the vessel has been turned out.

The launch was on Monday and in keeping with such an auspicious occasion; the metrological conditions were at their best. In anticipation of the event a large assemblage of towns people had gathered at the foot of Peel Hill and round the neighbourhood of the builder's yard. Mr. and Mrs. Egner were among those present. An exceptionally suitable high tide prevailed, and everything favoured a successful launch. All the morning the builders staff had been kept busy making preparations, and just before noon the last of the wedges were knocked away, and Peel's newest drifter slid gracefully and smoothly down the ways, taking the water in the most satisfactory manner. As the drifter commenced to move away, Mrs Egner, the wife of the owner, named her the "Manx Bride."

The new drifter is slightly smaller than the "Manx Princess," but is built similarly strong and efficient. The measurements are: - 85 feet overall, 72 feet keel, 18 feet beam. The lines are equally elegant, and should develop a good speed. As soon as ready the "Manx Bride" is to be towed to the Clyde by the "Manx Princess," there to have the engines fitted by Messrs. McKee and Baxter, of Govan, who gave such satisfaction in the engine equipment of the "Manx. Princess." The coal consumption will be less. The "Manx. Bride" will be lit by acetylene gas, and will have the latest improvements in gearing.

It is gratifying to know that a well-respected Peel man - Mr. James Crellin, of Stanley Road - is to be the master.

We sincerely trust that Mr. Egner will find his new possession so highly remunerative an investment that we shall soon see a third on the stocks.

The story continued on January 21st 1911, when the following appeared - "It is very pleasing to note that at least one of the Peel industries is at present kept busy. Shipbuilding is in full swing. On Thursday there was launched from the yard of Messrs. Neakle and Watterson, a nobby for a Dingle owner. The launch was effected very successfully. The boat is a nice model of the usual design for which the firm is famous, and her dimensions are 45 feet over all. The firm are at present constructing a motor fishing boat for Arklow. Pressure of work necessitated the firm refusing an order of a steam drifter for Scotland, they being unable to guarantee delivery in time."

Moving on to April 8th 1911 it was stated - " On Saturday morning last there was launched from the yard of Messrs. Neakle and Watterson, a motor nobby for Arklow. The vessel is 55 feet over all, and 16 feet beam, and is a nicely lined boat, and up to the usual standard for which the firm is noted. She will be fitted with a Bolinder motor engine. The firm have still a number of orders.

The next report referred to the trials of this vessel and this was reported on May 13th 1911 - "Much interest has been manifested in the trials of the motor-fitted fishing boat recently launched from a Peel yard. She is built for an Arklow owner and is named the "Hidden Treasure." The engines, which are of a new character as far as Peel is concerned. She made her first trial across the bay and back, on Wednesday with between 80 to 90 people on board, and gave every satisfaction. On Thursday morning another trial was given with equally good results. Heywood Bros. of Belfast supplied the engine. The work of completing the vessel is being rapidly pushed on, and she will most likely be ready to proceed to her destination in a week."

While on June 3rd 1911 the following report - "On Saturday there was launched from the boat building yard of Messrs. Neakle and Watterson, a nobby built to the order of Mr. Jeremiah O'Connor, of Dingle, Southern Ireland. The boat, which is named "Ocean Billow", is a nice lined model, and quite up to the usual standard for which this firm is noted. She is 46 feet over-all and has a 13 feet beam. The vessel is now nearly completed, and will shortly sail for her destination. The firm have still in hand two orders for Ireland, one of which is for a motor boat."

Then on July 13th. 1911 - "A very successful launch was accomplished at the yard of Messrs. Neakle and Watterson on Wednesday at noon. There was some uncertainty up to the last moment as to whether the launch should take place, owing to the lowness of the tide, which was however, the highest for the month. In view of the fact that it would have to be postponed for a fortnight it was decided that the launch should take place. Matters were so well arranged that very little inconvenience be caused by the lowness of the tide. The boat, which is beautifully shaped, is a nobby, built to the order of an owner from Portavogie, County Down, Northern Ireland. She is 45 feet over-all, with a $12^1/_2$ feet beam, and is named "Kindly Light." She is to be ready to sail for her destination on about the middle of next week..

While on September 2nd 1911 it was reported that another launch had taken place at the yard of Messrs. Neakle and Watterson on the previous Saturday. It was a nobby for a Dingle owner. She was of a shapely design being 46 feet over-all, with a 13 beam, and was fitted with a 12 - 15 h.p. Skandia motor engine. This was the first motor fishing boat by the firm for Dingle. It was expected that the fitting of the engine and the final touches would be completed by the middle of the month.

Another successful launch was reported on October 28th 1911. It took place at the yard of Messrs. Neakle and Watterson the previous Tuesday, and was a nobby built for a Cashircaveen (Ireland), owner. The boat was 45 feet over-all, and a 13 beam, a neat model.

The next report was on March 9th 1912 - "On Tuesday there was launched from the yard of Messrs. Neakle and Watterson, a beautiful and well shaped fishing boat, built to the order of Messrs. Caulfield and Richard, of Howth, Ireland. The launch was a great success, the boat taking the water most gracefully. The vessel is 60 feet over-all, and a 17 feet beam, and 50 feet on the keel. She is to be fitted with a 60 h.p. Gardiner motor engine. The firm still have several orders on hand, one being a small yacht for a Manchester owner and a barge for Douglas.

Then on May 12th 1912 - "A most successful and well executed launch took place from the Peel Mill yard of Messrs. Neakle and Watterson on Saturday morning, when a yacht built to the order of Mr. Sawley Brown, of Manchester, gracefully took the water. As the vessel glided down the ways, she was christened by the breaking of a bottle of wine, the ceremony being successfully performed by Ada Kaighin, youngest daughter of Mr. J. Kaighin, Derby House, Station Place, Peel. The yacht is a neat and shapely craft measuring 39 feet over-all and 11 feet beam. She is fitted with a 15 h.p. three cylinder Gardiner engine. She will make Fleetwood her headquarters.

Moving to June 15th 1912, it was revealed - "The motor fishing boat recently built for Howth, by Messrs. Neakle and Watterson, is now ready for delivery, her crew have arrived, and on Thursday the 60 h.p. Gardiner engine was tried by a trip to sea. A number of interested passengers were on board. The boat and the engines gave every satisfaction.

It was revealed on July 6th 1912 of the successful launching of a large barge the previous Monday. The vessel was to be utilised for the landing and embarking of passengers on the steam ferries at the Battery Pier, Douglas. Miss Gladys Brown, of Douglas, performed the christening ceremony; the name given was the "Cushag." The vessel was very strongly built to withstand the frequent shocks of the ferry steamers coming alongside. The Tyrconnel towed round the barge to Douglas on July 8th. 1912.

A further launch took place on January 9th 1913, it being a fishing yacht built to the order of Messrs. J and C and H Cowell, of Bridge Street, Peel. The vessel was a strong shapely craft and measures 47 feet over all, with beam of 13 feet. The vessel was to be used for long-line fishing.

At that time the firm had had an order for a vessel for a similar purpose for Mr. W. Crellin, of Shore road.

The next report of May 24th 1913 revealed two launches. The first was on Tuesday previous when a new nobby, which was greatly admired and built to the order of Mr. G. Gaskell, Patrick Street, Peel, gracefully took the water. She was named the "White Heather," a trim craft with the appearance of being a fast boat. She was 46 feet over all, with a 14-foot beam. She was to be fitted with an auxiliary Kelvin motor of 15-20 h.p.

Miss Florrie Sherstone, of Sheffield, who was staying in Peel, performed the christening ceremony. When the vessel was fitted, her trials proved very satisfactory, and attained a speed of 12 m.p.h., with nets, etc., aboard. She made her first trip to the herring fishing grounds two days later.

The second launch took place on May 21st 1913, it was a neat half-decked yacht, which was built for Mr. Lea, Birmingham. This vessel was 44 feet over-all, and 12'/₂ feet beam. She was also fitted with an auxiliary Kelvin motor engine of 0-12 h.p.

Moving to October 4th 1913 it was reported that a very successful launch had been conducted the previous Wednesday when a half-decker yacht built to the order of Mr. Wm. Crellin, Peel. The vessel was a beautiful model measuring 46 feet over-all, with a 13 beam, and was to be used for the line fishing all year round.

At that time the firm were fitting the "Gien Mie," the half-decker belonging to Cowell Bros. with a Kelvin motor.

The next report appeared on March 21st 1914 when it was revealed that a launch had taken place the previous Saturday. It was a beautiful lined boat built to the order of Messrs. J and J Canapa, Douglas. The vessel was 55 feet over-all, with a beam of 15 feet. She was to be fitted with twin motors and was to be used as a passenger boat between Douglas and Port Soderick.

While on May 14th. 1914 it was reported that the Neakle and Watterson yard had launched on the previous Monday, a barge built to the order of the Douglas Steam Ferries Ltd. The barge was to be moored alongside the Victoria Pier, and used for the embarkation and disembarkation of passengers. The vessel was 60 feet over all, with a beam of 16 feet. She was constructed for the most part of oak, and cost about £500. The christening ceremony was performed by Miss Miriam Elizabeth Clarke, granddaughter of Mr. David Clarke, Peveril House, one of the directors, was also present. Others present were Mr. And Mrs. Ewart Crellin, and Miss Clarke. During the ceremony referred in eulogistic terms to the work done by the firm, they two years ago having made a barge for the company, which is in use on the Douglas Head side of the harbour.

Then on August 1st 1914 it was reported that the firm had successfully launched a nobby-rigged boat the previous Saturday. It was built to the order of the Department of Agriculture and Technical Instruction Fisheries Branch, Ireland, for Mr. Kavanagh of Arklow. The vessel was the sister to the vessel built by the yard three of four years ago, and was named the "Lucy Mary." The vessel was 57 feet over-all with a beam of 16 feet. She was to be fitted with a 40 h.p. Bolinder engine.

From this period on to the end of the First World War in 1918, there is very little information available, but the yard did carry on working with a very depleted staff as most of the men were serving in the armed forces or merchant navy. Most of the work they did do was repair work.

During the war the Admiralty offered the firm work in repairing minesweepers, but this work they declined as they felt that they would not be able to carry out the work due to the limited number of staff available.

The period just after the war was, of course, a very difficult one, as the fishing fleet had been greatly depleted as all the young men had been serving in the forces, and on their return did not wish to go back to the fishing due to its hazards.

There was only one reference to the shipbuilders in the following year and that was on July 19th 1919 it being as follows - "While coming alongside Peel breakwater, the drifter "Berrie Braes," which was on her way to base for demobilisation, bumped into the breakwater through engine trouble, and sprung her stern. The vessel was in the charge of skipper Hy. Cannon, of Peel. The necessary repairs being carried out by Messrs. Neakle and Watterson, of Peel.

The failure to revive the fishing not only caused concern for those involved, but also by the Government of the time, and this concern was reflected in a request by the Governor for ideas on how to bring about a revival. About the same time a prospectus was published seeking capital for a new company "The Manx Fishing Industries Limited."

As a result of the Governor's appeal, the government of the Island came forward with a scheme, which offered loans on very easy terms to fishermen and others to build new boats and equipment for fishing.

Although the firm seemed to be ticking over the only reference to its activities was on September 18th 1920, it being - "Last week there was launched from the yard of Messrs. Neakle and Watterson a most serviceable motor boat suitable either for private touring or for hire, either by charter or for day trips. The vessel is 30 feet over all, with a beam of 7 feet and she is fitted with a 7 - 9 h.p. Kelvin engine. The decks are of teak. She has a fore cabin saloon, a covered engine room, and a cockpit. There is also a well between the engine room and the fore cabin, and there is an alleyway from the aft cockpit through the engine room to the saloon. In addition to motor power, sails can be used; the vessel is being rigged for a foresail and mainsail. She is named "Lheannan Shee."

There is a blank patch in information concerning the firm during 1921 and 1922 and it was not until May 5th. 1923, and this was as follows - "Messrs. Neakle and Watterson, boat builders, Peel, have just completed a motor launch to the order of Mr. G. S. Dean, of Port Erin. She is a beautifully modelled boat, and is a very seaworthy vessel. She is 22 feet over all, with a beam of $6^{1}/_{2}$ feet. She is fitted with a 6 - 7 h.p, two cylinder Kelvin engine. She has teak top strikes and combings. The boat is for private use and will be used for cruising and fishing. She is a very attractive looking boat and is up to the very high standard for which the firm is noted."

Although there was a long period of depression during the 1920's and 1930's the firm continued to operate and build some very fine vessels, and some of these are still in use to day.

In the latter part of the firms existence most of the boats built were of the small or medium sized boats which were suitable for fishing or for pleasure, and they all had very fine lines.

The firm had moved across the river when Watson's vacated it and it was here the firm finally ended its operation.

It was a point of interest that the vessel "Gien Mie" built by this firm for Cowell Bros., of Peel, who later sold it to Mr Dixon, of Whitehaven, and then he sold it to American owners, and it was taken to Montreal, Canada in February 1937. She was 37 feet over-all, and 13 feet beam. Another of the larger fishing boats was the "Manx Shearwater."

It is interesting to note that this firm were pioneers in the use of the canoe stern, which became popular for motor boats, and it was generally copied.

The end of the firm came as a result of the death of one of the partners, Mr William Watterson, on July 9th, 1939, at the age of 70 years. He was a skilled draughtsman as well as being a builder, and his designs were, particularly in the early days of the firm, revolutionary, which gave their boats that little extra speed to make them very special. Mr Neakle was also a skilled craftsman, and the result of this combination made their craft a pride to behold with their outstanding character, design, seaworthiness, and workmanship.

These two gentlemen spent a great deal of their lives together, having worked as partners for 42 years, and with the closing of this yard, it was the end of an era in shipbuilding that added greatly to the prosperity of Peel, where the boats were built that could compete with any in the world for their seaworthiness and workmanship.

'Manx Bride'

Chapter Eight

The River Neb

The River Neb means great or big river and it joins the sea through Peel harbour. Like many other rivers on the Island it at one time abounded with fish right up to the middle of the 19th. century. This, however, was brought to a halt when the workings at Foxdale mines were expanded which resulted in pollution and this either killed or drove away the fish. One of the popular areas was the top of the harbour to Glenfaba Bridge and the method most widely used for this type of fishing at that time was the ancient method of spearing the fish. The implement used was called a lister and consisted of a three-pronged fork with a long handle.

During the early part of the 19th century there was an old character living in Peel who was only known as Old Billy Sam, and, who lived by his wits. He took parties of visitors round the Castle and also tours of the hill from time to time did the odd job. However, there was one thing he was an expert on, and that was the use of a lister. He visited this area regularly, and one day he saw a salmon in the river. Billy threw the lister, which pierced the salmon and one of the prongs went through the fish, and the 'lug' of a griddle that was lying on the bed beneath the salmon.

However, the story did not end there, because, when Billy Sam threw his prize ashore, the griddle fell into a gorse bush, and killed a hare in its form. Thus old Billy Sam secured the salmon, and a hare, at one throw of the lister.

Kelsall's Kipper Houses

Just below the site of the old shipyards and right opposite the present bridge is a fish processing plant. The buildings were erected in 1882, and at that time they were the most up-to-date kipper houses and curing yard in Peel. These premises were built for a firm known as Kelsall's who came to the Island each year to cure herring and produce Manx kippers most of which were exported for sale in England.

The business ran successfully throughout the early part of the 20th century right up to the 1930's when the business changed hands and this resulted in the closing of the Peel operation. However, Messrs. T. Moore and Sons Limited purchased the premises, which moved their processing operations from Michael Street to these premises where they operated successfully until 1989. The business of kipper curing has carried on here today, which is run by Paul Desmond who also runs the business as a Kipper Museum with daily tours.

Kelsall's Kipper Factory

The Bridges

Up to 1883 there was only a low footbridge across the harbour, and as there was no through road along the quay it only gave access to the hill. It was situated about 20 feet lower than the present bridge, and was known as Clarke's Bridge, taking the name from the builder.

The present bridge was originally built as part of the harbour development of that time. The Isle of Man Harbour Board rebuilt the bridge in 1938 when it was widened and strengthened.

Neb Road

There was a section of road, which has now been incorporated as part of the quay, and which was known as the Neb Road. It consisted of the section of the road running from the bridge to a slipway that carried the blackwoods and ran between the harbour and the railway station. The blackwoods was a form of bridge joining the section running alongside the railway station to the road on the other side and was a short cut saving for people coming from Mill Road. It consisted of a series of thick planks in pairs linked with supports for the full distance and was about 18 inches wide that made it difficult to pass on them.

The Red Herring House

Just below the junction of Mill Road and the Neb Road stood a large building, which was a red herring house, which was known in the latter part of the 18th century as Ellison's.

The red herring was the forerunner of the kipper. At that time girls aged from nine to thirteen years carried the herrings in baskets from the boats to the various curing houses. On reaching the premises the herring were thoroughly rubbed with salt and piled regularly with a layer of salt between each row, then left for a few days to purify. They were then washed, and, when the water was sufficiently drained from them, were fixed by the mouth on small rods, and hung up in the extensive houses built for the purpose.

The red herring houses were very high; in length exceeding thirty yards, and in width about twenty. The length was divided into several spaces, and here the herring-rods were hung, reaching in rows from the roof of the house to within eight feet from the floor. Underneath, several fires were kindled of dried roots of oak, which were continually kept smoking for four to five weeks. When the herring were sufficiently reddened, they were taken down and barrelled, and shipped.

This house appeared to change hands quite a lot during the early part of the 19th century. Corris's map of 1784 showed it as Ellison's. Later Caesar Corris had it, while in February, 1813, it was advertised for sale by auction, and again in 1814 and 1815, Messrs. Holmes, of Douglas, eventually took it over, and for many years cured herring there. Then the Graves family took the premises over and eventually sold it to the Railway Company who demolished it to extend the station.

The Lake

Part of the site of the old railway station was a lake that was kept filled by the tide, but gradually the site was filled up and the land reclaimed to enlarge the railway station.

One of Peel's shipyards of the mid 19th century was on the banks of the lake and was known as Tom Cowell's. This yard specialised in smaller vessels and repairs. The vessels were launched into the lake and after they were fitted and rigged were sailed out at high tide. When boats needed repairs they were taken in at high tide. However, if they were too big there was a cradle or dry dock alongside the quay where the repairs were carried out.

At the time of Tom Cowell's death there were three ships on the stocks in the yard, and it was probably when these were completed that this yard was closed down.

The Railway Station

Peel was the first town on the Island to have a direct link with Douglas by rail, even though this was not the site originally chosen by the company, as they intended to bring the line across the present golf links and to site the station on a level with Albany Road, but after discussions with the citizens of Peel, it was decided to come into Peel along the river. The main reason for this was easy access for the export of fish and also for the transport of goods brought in by boat or to be taken away by boat.

The original station was only a small affair when the waiting room and the refreshment room and ticket office faced the harbour and at that time painted Indian red and stone colour. The refreshment room was licensed to sell liquor, and it had a cellar for the storage of wine, etc. Unfortunately there was a problem with the cellar, as when the tide was high the cellar man needed his Wellington boots to go down as there was always six or seven inches of water and on very high tides considerably more.

The official opening of the line took place on Thursday, May 1st 1873, and the public opening, held on Thursday 1st July 1873. An interesting feature of the return journey was that it only took $27^1/2$ minutes. The second train the day of the public opening carried 500 people to Peel. Regular public services started on the 2nd July 1873. The receipts for the first five weeks were £1,735-16-7d.

In the 1890's a fire burned part of the wooden building which was replaced temporarily. Then in 1904 a further fire burned the buildings right down too and temporary buildings were used until 1907 when the buildings alongside Station Place were built and contained the ticket office, refreshment rooms, and waiting rooms.

During the First World War a branch line was run down the quay for the purpose of transporting goods brought in for the Knockaloe camp, but this was removed in the 1920's.

The line was closed in the 1950's and was reopened in 1962 but this lasted only a few years before it was closed forever, and only the station building remains, which now forms part of the House of Mannanan, to reflect the past.

The Railway Hotel

Situated on the Station Place is the Creek Inn which is an early Victorian building with its iron balconies etc. and in its early days it was known as the "Oddfellows' Arms," then with the coming of the railway it eventually became known as the "Railway Hotel," however, when the station closed it was decided to change the name, taking the name of the area it is situated "The Creek Inn."

PEEL CASTLE, I. O. M. FROM SHORE.

Chapter Nine

The Brewery - Net Loft - Net Factory

The large building known as the Viking Longhouse is about 250 years old and was shown on Corris's Map of 1784 as a brewery. Little is known of its early history, but the Teare family owned it. On the same map, there is shown a small landing platform possibly for the unloading of hops for the making of beer, and loading of the finished product for export, as beer was one of the things that the Island did export during the 18th century and early 19th century.

In the early part of the 19th century it was said that this brewery did one brew a week. About this period the building was extended to include what is now the house alongside. They were inter-connected with doors on the first and second floors. Old photographs show that there were doors on each floor of this section in the centre of it, similar to the main building and other warehouses in Peel. However, this section was converted into a house and shop that had a liquor licence in the 1870's. In the 1880's the brewery was closed and the equipment was sold by public auction.

However, the building was still retained by the Teare family who converted the building into a net loft, and the brewing pans were converted into barking pans for the darkening and preservation of fishing nets. And these were still in use right up to the 1960's.

Then in 1910 part of the premises was used as a net factory when Mr. Teare purchased some treadle net making machines for the manufacture of nets, as at that time there were no net factories operating following the decline of the fishing.

Part of the first floor was used for the storage of net belonging to the Teare fleet of boats, and each of the boats had their own part with the name of the boat written in chalk on the beam above.

All nets were carefully checked by women who then took them to the floor above, where they were spread out, and the necessary repairs carried out and in some cases this meant putting a whole new section or jeebin, as they were called in.

With the decline of the fishing the building was used for other purposes. The Peel Water Company as a store used the ground floor for many years until they moved to more suitable premises. Then it became a store for a fish merchant for a number of years. The first floor was used for many years as a builders store in fact, right up to the time the building was last sold. The second floor was a rifle range for a while and it was also used by the Peel Sea Cadets for quite a few years.

The building was eventually purchased by the Peel Vikings who had been using part of the building as a store for their equipment for a number of years. They repaired the ground floor and covered the barking pans to make a solid floor. They also put in toilet facilities and made the rest of the floor into a store. The first floor they converted into a Viking Longhouse, which had been a tourist attraction for a number of years. More recently they converted the second floor into a banqueting hall, which was opened by His Excellency the Lieutenant Governor in 1982, and was hoped that that too would be a tourist attraction. The first floor was then used as a nightclub.

The building was eventually sold to a local building developer, Jonathan Irving of Street Heritage, who is converting it into a block of luxury apartments and retail outlets.

Graves Shipyard

With the development of shipbuilding throughout the Island in the early part of the 19th century the Graves family, who were already successful merchants, added shipbuilding to their activities. They set up their yard just below the Viking Longhouse where is situated a large vault which they used as a store for their goods as merchants.

The head of the family business at that time was Thomas Joshua Graves and the shipbuilding side proved highly successful and they developed rapidly with the opening of a second yard on the other side of St. Peter's Lane. They built many fine ships here, from very small fishing boats to large schooners..

The yard ran successfully right up to 1897 when the health of Henry Graves failed, but the yard was taken over by Messrs. Neakle and Watterson, who continued where the Graves family left off until they moved to a more suitable site in 1908.

When the vault was sealed up the Graves family used the site for their coal merchants section of the business which they ran until the early 1900's when it was sold, and there was a coal merchant operating from this site right up to the turn of the 21st century.

During the smuggling era in the latter part of the 18th century there was a network of tunnels running from this vault, and the theory handed down from the past is that it was connected by a tunnel to the vaults lower down the quay, and there were branches running all round the town, right up Douglas Street to Atholl Street, Atholl Place and the Shore Road.

St. Peter's Lane

Prior to 1871 when the lane was renamed "St. Peter's Lane.," it was known by several names "Church Lane," "Vault's Lane" and "Sumner's Lane."

Nan Sumner ran the inn that stood halfway up the lane, the building being demolished in the early 1960's, and the area now contains a garage. The inn was very popular during the early part of the 19th century and was noted for its festive board in the 1830's, when it was claimed to be the best at that time.

Opposite were a number of cottages for people who worked at the brewery and later at the net lofts and net factory and were owned by the Teare family.

Keown's Lane

There was a lane running at the back of Castle Street from St. Peter's Lane to the Quay, which was prior to 1810 the only through way along the Quay. Most of the area from Crown Street to St. Peter's Lane was a large grass bank where many boats were dragged up for the winter where work could be carried out in preparation for the next season.

Up to quite recent times the entrance to the lane was narrow and twisted as there was a cottage with a garden and opposite there was a very small house consisting of two stories - one room on each floor. These two buildings have now been demolished making access through, easy.

Peel Sailor's Shelter and Fisherman's Refuge

There were tremendous changes in the pattern of fishing from the 1850's on including a great expansion in the fleet that meant that over 1500 men were engaged in this fleet. While the bulk came from Peel and the surrounding areas, they were supplemented by men from other parts of the Island such as Douglas and Ramsey. As these men could not get home during the week it was felt that there was a need for a place where they could spend their spare time.

The idea of forming a "Peel Sailor's Shelter and Fisherman's Refuge" was being formulated by High Bailiff Robert Moore, who on October 12th 1876, issued a circular, embodying a scheme having for its immediate object the establishment of a comfortable resort "for intercourse and improvement," and would be available for "a general meeting, smoking, and reading room."

The scheme as propounded, was at once, in the most enthusiastic manner, taken up, not only by those for whom benefit it was suggested, but by the general public throughout the Island.

A week after the scheme was first announced a public meeting was held on October 18th 1876, and the institution was established. The officials elected were - Hon. Secretary, Mr W. Kinvig; Hon. Treasurer, Mr James Morrison; Committee - Messrs. Robert J. Moore, Henry M. Graves, William Fargher and Robert Corrin.

The committee decided that it was advisable to erect a suitable building instead of renting a room as a temporary measure. A subscription list was opened, and this received ready and liberal support.

The main difficulty facing the committee was finding a suitable site, and this was eventually overcome by a generous offer by the Isle of Man Harbour Commissioners. They agreed to lease a portion of their land, 44 feet in length and 22 feet in breadth, for ten years at a nominal rent of one shilling per annum.

With regard to the structure, the committee purchased a number of good second hand windows and doors, together with a quantity of timber that had been used in connection with the harbour works, adopted a plan and invited estimates for the erection of a building to cover the whole of the ground acquired from the Harbour Commissioners.

The tender of Mr. Daniel Anderson was accepted, and work begun, with a foundation brick. The foundation stone being laid by Mrs. E. Moore, on 9th December 1876. Due to the speed the contractor worked, the building, formed of brick laid in a frame-work of timber, with corrugated roof, was formally opened on 12th January 1877. The whole cost was £172-17s-2½d and the subscriptions contributed amounted to £156-12s-0d leaving a small deficit which was eventually cleared.

The shelter also received many gifts of books, maps, and newspapers, which made it a place where the fishermen could go and spend their leisure time, whether it was for a read, a smoke, a chat, or play draughts, dominoes, crib or other card games.

During the remaining years of his life, High Bailiff Robert Moore devoted a great deal of his time and energy in promoting the shelter and raising funds for it. Perhaps it was fitting that the last public function he attended prior to his death in 1884 was a lecture in the Sailor's Shelter to raise funds for it.

The Shelter appeared to be run with reasonable success until about 1894 when it appeared to run out of funds, plus the fact that many of those who set the wheels in motion had died and as a result the Shelter was closed.

It remained closed until 1904, when efforts were made to have it re-opened and this proved to be successful. As the old agreement with the Harbour Commissioners had lapsed, a new one for a much longer period was drawn up and agreed upon. A new committee was also appointed, and a fund raising scheme promoted. This saw the Shelter firmly on its feet and it has continued to run ever since.

The premises were renovated and events were held there regularly. Perhaps one of the most popular events organised during the early part of the 20th century was the community hymn singing every Sunday evening when the Shelter was filled to capacity and there was often standing room only. There were also lantern lectures, concerts, and whist drives, which proved valuable revenue for the maintenance and running of the premises.

With the decline of the fishing fleet and the changing pattern of life, the use of the Shelter has also changed, but it has been adapted for the changing scene and it is there, always available when it is needed.